Cities in the Metaverse

Cities in the Metaverse offers a comprehensive exploration of the intersection between urban environments and digital realms. The book examines:

- The size and shape of cities in the Metaverse
- Spatial computing and its impact on digital interaction
- Digital twins in urban planning and management
- Avatars and social dynamics in virtual spaces
- Economic models emerging in the Metaverse
- The influence of gaming on immersive digital landscapes
- The impact of Artificial Intelligence on the Metaverse
- Potential futures of digital habitation

Drawing from architecture, computer science, urban planning, geography, social studies, and economics, the authors provide a multidisciplinary analysis of how virtual cities are shaping our digital future. Using key case studies, they trace the evolution from early cyberspace concepts to current spatial computing technologies, offering insights into both historical context and future possibilities. The book addresses key questions about the opportunities and challenges presented by Metaverse technologies, including issues of accessibility, creativity, and the future of humans and artificial intelligence co-existing, side by side, in digital spaces. It serves as a practical guide, equipping readers with the knowledge they need to navigate the future of urban life in virtual environments with a thought-provoking examination of how we might build, inhabit, and govern cities in the Metaverse.

The authors explore the concept of digital twins, demonstrating how these virtual replicas of physical spaces can revolutionise urban planning and management. They delve into the social aspects of the Metaverse, examining how avatars shape our interactions and relationships in digital realms. Economic considerations are central to the book ethos, with an analysis of emerging models that often leverage blockchain technologies. The book addresses the challenges, potential pitfalls, and ethical considerations in creating and inhabiting digital cities. At the same time, it takes a step back and examines already abandoned digital worlds, offering lessons from past attempts at creating virtual spaces.

Essential reading for urban planners, geographers, economists, technologists, policymakers, and anyone interested in the future of cities and digital interaction, *Cities in the Metaverse* provides a balanced, informed perspective on this rapidly evolving field.

The Metaverse

The Metaverse
A Critical Introduction
David Burden & Maggi Savin-Baden

The Metaverse for Learning and Education
Maggi Savin-Baden & David Burden

Cities in the Metaverse
Spatial Computing, Digital Twins, Avatars, Economics, and Digital Habitation on the New Frontier
Andrew Hudson-Smith, Duncan Wilson and Valerio Signorelli

For more information about this series please visit: https://www.routledge.com/The-Metaverse/book-series/

Cities in the Metaverse

Spatial Computing, Digital Twins, Avatars, Economics and Digital Habitation on the New Frontier

Andrew Hudson-Smith,
Duncan Wilson, and Valerio Signorelli

CRC Press
Taylor & Francis Group
Boca Raton London New York

CRC Press is an imprint of the
Taylor & Francis Group, an **informa** business
A CHAPMAN & HALL BOOK

Designed cover image: Andrew Hudson-Smith

First edition published 2025
by CRC Press
2385 NW Executive Center Drive, Suite 320, Boca Raton FL 33431

and by CRC Press
4 Park Square, Milton Park, Abingdon, Oxon, OX14 4RN

CRC Press is an imprint of Taylor & Francis Group, LLC

ISBN: 978-1-032-57670-1 (hbk)
ISBN: 978-1-032-57669-5 (pbk)
ISBN: 978-1-003-44043-7 (ebk)

DOI: 10.1201/9781003440437

Typeset in Palatino
by KnowledgeWorks Global Ltd.

Contents

About the Authors

Andrew Hudson-Smith is a Professor of Digital Urban Systems at the Centre for Advanced Spatial Analysis (CASA), University College London. He focuses on real-time data, virtual environments and the Internet of Things within the urban environment. He is also an elected Fellow of the Royal Society of Arts, a Fellow of the Academy of Social Sciences and a Fellow of the Royal Geographic Society. Socials: @digitalurban

Duncan Wilson is a Professor of Connected Environments at the Centre for Advanced Spatial Analysis (CASA), University College London. His research focuses on how emerging technologies, such as connected sensors and cognitive computing, can augment our understanding of the built and natural environment. He has over 25 years of experience in industry and is a Fellow of the Royal Society of Arts. Socials: @djdunc

Valerio Signorelli is a Lecturer in Connected Environments at the Bartlett Centre for Advanced Spatial Analysis (CASA), University College London. He holds an MSc in Architecture and Urban Design and a PhD in Territorial Design and Government from the Department of Architecture and Urban Studies at the Politecnico di Milano (Italy). He is also a Fellow of the Royal Society of Arts. Socials: @ValeSignorelli

Introduction

He is not seeing real people, of course. This is all a part of the moving illustration drawn by his computer according to the specifications coming down the fibre-optic cable. The people are pieces of software called avatars. They are the audio-visual bodies that people use to communicate with each other in the Metaverse.

Neal Stephenson, Snow Crash (1992), p. 35

In the digital realm beyond the confines of the physical world, a new frontier is emerging, known as the Metaverse. This immersive digital landscape encompasses millions of human operated avatars, representations of human form in digital space, existing alongside Artificial Intelligence (AI)-controlled avatars known as bots. Together, these avatars are constructing intricate and expansive worlds that transcend the limitations of reality, existing within a vast network of computers. In essence, digital brick by brick, they are building small hamlets, villages, towns, and sprawling cities populated by millions of people and existing entirely in the Metaverse.

Defining the Metaverse poses a challenge, as multiple interpretations exist. In its fully realised state, it is primarily characterised as a distributed, multi-user, interactive, social, shared, subjective, and persistent three-dimensional digital experience. It offers a space where individuals can create and engage in limitless activities unconstrained by conventional physical laws. The Metaverse represents a significant advancement in our ability to interact within and with digital systems and other people. It shifts away from the objective individual window-and-mouse interface towards a more subjective first-person social experience. In this realm, the "interface" seamlessly integrates with the virtual environment, mirroring the natural interactions found in physical space. An emerging term for this is spatial computing.

The terminology of the Metaverse has recently entered the public's awareness, partly as a result of Facebook's rebranding in 2021 to Meta and their subsequent efforts to create an occupied Metaverse. However, the development of Metaverses has been ongoing since the early 1990s. This book examines examples of Metaverses that we, the authors, and others have developed, encompassing expansive worlds of bots, friendships, economics, relationships, and cityscapes. Before exploring these worlds, it is essential to acknowledge the prevailing trends in the broader built environment and technology professions. Digital twins are one of the current primary driving forces in the field of the Built Environment.

The concept of a digital twin emerged during a presentation by Dr Grieves at the University of Michigan in 2002, associated with product manufacturing. Dr Grieves's concept entailed linking digital representations of manufactured products to their physical counterparts throughout their life cycle through a digital twin concept model. According to Grieves (2015), the model comprised three main elements: (a) physical products in Real Space, (b) Virtual Products in Virtual Space, and (c) the data and information connections linking the virtual and real products. As such, it is a mix of the real world, a 3D model of the real world, adding this model to digital space, and linking data from the real world back into the digital model—creating a digital twin of things, places, and spaces.

Moreover, the concept of digital twins can also be linked to the "Mirror World" concept initially proposed by David Gelernter (1991) in his influential work titled Mirror Worlds: Or the Day Software Puts the Universe in a Shoebox. Gelernter (1991) defined "mirror worlds" as software models of a particular portion of reality, a segment of the real world occurring "outside your window," which can be represented digitally and then repeatedly rescaled into a form that allows for entry and manipulation. A mirror world is anchored in a specific real space, and its power lies in how we manipulate the reality it represents, extending its connections beyond a singular physical product to encompass broader environments and spaces. Gelernter (1991) predicted that

> *a software model of your city, once established, will be available (like a public park) to as many interested parties as possible ... it will sustain a multitude of diverse perspectives... each visitor will zoom in, pan around, and traverse the model at their discretion.*
>
> **(Roush 2007)**

This foundation underpins the digital twin concept, a mirror of the world rendered in software and occupied by individuals who log into the system, resulting in a collaborative multi-user digital space. When connected to economic and social factors, this space gives rise to the concept of a living, breathing Metaverse.

Within the world of technology, there is always a rolling frontier, a place where the forefront of developments take place. They are occupied and used by people wanting to try out the latest and greatest before they become mainstream. Today, that frontier is arguably within Spatial Computing and headsets such as the Vision Pro by Apple and the Meta Quest by Meta, headsets that transport their users into augmented and virtual reality (VR) worlds. Back in the mid to late 1990s, this frontier was known as "Cyberspace," a term that is now rarely used, yet only 20 years ago it was one of the most popular terms used to define the size, depth, and content of the Internet. The term was first coined by Gibson (1984) in his science fiction novel Neuromancer, in which he defined it as not really a place, not really a space, but a notional space—

> *A consensual hallucination experienced daily by billions of legitimate operators in every nation, a graphic representation of data abstracted from the banks of every computer in the human system. Unthinkable complexity. Lines of light ranged in the nonspace of the mind, clusters and constellations of data like city lights receding....*
>
> **(Gibson 1984, p. 57)**

These city lights receding are used as the loading screen for one of many Metaverse systems, known as "Oncyber," to display their loading page, moving and teleporting between environments. Indeed, at the time of writing, there are over 170 companies building the Metaverse, making it not a single unit but a series of worlds interlinked and intertwined by the concepts of space and place within the Internet. Throughout this book, we will refer to a myriad of companies building space within the Internet, from early pioneers known as ActiveWorlds Corporation through to one of the largest and most historically successful, Second Life, and the current wave of VR platforms such as VR Chat, Spatial.io, Oncyber, and the now sadly now defunct Altspace VR and Mozilla Hubs.

As we stand on the cusp of this new era, looking into three-dimensional and augmented worlds ahead of us, the potential offered by spatial computing, digital twins, avatars, and new and emerging economic models is vast. In this book, we embark on an in-depth exploration of the virtual cities created by spatial computing platforms and examine their multifaceted implications and possibilities. The book navigates as yet uncharted territory through an interdisciplinary approach that synthesises the disciplines of architecture, computer science, urban planning, social studies, and economics as we venture into the future of urban existence: Cities in the Metaverse.

As we embark on this exploration, it is prudent to recall the cycles of heightened anticipation and subsequent disillusionment that have historically characterised attempts to realise this concept. In the late 1990s, virtual worlds offered us our first widespread glimpse into what a fully immersive digital society might entail. Cyberspace became synonymous with the Metaverse, and with the advent of software known as Avatars, there was palpable excitement for a time. It appeared as though we stood on the cusp of a new era, an era that has gone full cycle through boom and bust. However, as is often the case with groundbreaking ideas, the reality could not live up to the utopian vision that its pioneers had promised. Technological constraints, socio-cultural barriers, and a lack of sustainable economic models caused these early endeavours to establish the Metaverse to fade from public attention. This resulted in the abandonment of worlds that had been constructed and inhabited digitally. Although physically unaltered and unaged, they now stand as desolate digital ghost towns on the periphery of what was once a thriving frontier. Despite their current state of abandonment, these metascapes of the past provide a record of human activity. Similar to digital archaeology but instead of delving back to Roman times, we need only scratch the surface to uncover remnants of these lost worlds. We open our digital archaeological trenches to explore these in the chapter "Abandoned Worlds at the End of the Metaverse."

Throughout the late 1990s and onwards to the early 2000s, following the widespread enthusiasm for the Metaverse, the concept transitioned from its initial prominence to an antiquated status, relegated to the realm of speculative fiction in the cyberpunk genre and consigned to the annals of digital history. However, in recent years, the Metaverse has experienced a remarkable resurgence, analogous to the mythical phoenix rising from its own ashes. This renaissance has been driven by a convergence of influential factors, including exponential advancements in technology, increased acceptance of digital lifestyles by society, and innovative economic models that often draw upon blockchain technologies, which we explore in depth in "Economics and Security of Digital Space."

Despite fluctuations in the level of public interest surrounding the Metaverse, the vision of an all-encompassing immersive digital reality has remained steadfast, driving continuous innovation and exploration. However, it is imperative that we approach this renewed enthusiasm with a critical eye, learning from the lessons of previous attempts. It is easy to become swept away by the waves of hype, overlooking the challenges and unintended consequences of our creations. Yet it is within these waves that the virtual settlements, from hamlets to cities, that we alluded to at the outset, are being constructed, a process as old as civilisation itself. From the ancient Mesopotamian ziggurats to the modernist marvels of the twentieth century, urban landscapes have functioned as mirrors, reflecting the values, aspirations, and technological prowess of our societies. Now, as we witness the inception or rebirth of the Metaverse, we find ourselves presented with an unparalleled opportunity to shape and inhabit virtual cities that are unconstrained by the physical limitations of our physical world. In "Cities and Avatars," we delve deeper into these Metascapes, exploring their unique characteristics and potential implications.

As we have noted, the prevailing trend in technology, depending on the time of reading this document, is known as Spatial Computing. This phenomenon involves the overlaying and merging of digital space with our physical environments, effectively bringing the Metaverse from a confined and two-dimensional screen into a fully immersive three-dimensional world. It is possible that in the years since the initial publication of this work in 2025, the term "Spatial Computing" may have become as aged as "Cyberspace" is today. More widely recognised terms are "Virtual Reality," and "Mixed Reality" which, similar to the Metaverse, have experienced fluctuating waves of popularity and are now entering a new phase through Spatial Computing. These advancements present novel avenues for creative expression and interaction, heralding a transformative era akin to the dawn of the internet. With the potential for digital representations of our real-world spaces, known as digital twins, we can replicate our cities within the virtual realm. This capability allows us to monitor, manage, and manipulate these virtual cities in ways previously deemed impossible. While the adage "Rome was not built in a day" holds true, in the digital realm, particularly when combined with advancements in Artificial Intelligence, it is possible to construct a city not in a day but in a matter of milliseconds, at least in terms of representation. We explore this aspect further in the chapter on Turing's Dream and the Metaverse.

As we progress, it is imperative to maintain an ongoing dialogue regarding the opportunities and challenges posed by these developments. Through thoughtful and informed discourse, we can collaboratively shape a Metaverse that upholds human dignity, nurtures creativity, and promotes equitable access. This book, therefore, serves not only as a contemplation on cities in the Metaverse but also as an invitation to engage in critical thinking, questioning, and imaginative exploration. As we venture into this bold and uncharted territory, it is our collective imagination that will shape its architecture, urban planning, policymaking, and citizenry.

Amidst the ebb and flow of hype, upturns, and downturns, there exists an enduring aspect of the Metaverse that has remained steady and driven its future. Occupied by hundreds of thousands or even millions of people, avatars, and inhabited spaces, gaming worlds constitute a significant part of the Metaverse. These vast three-dimensional virtual landscapes, accessible through desktops, consoles, or VR headsets, provide players with opportunities not only for entertainment but also for socialisation and exploration. We delve deeper into this phenomenon in the chapter entitled "Playing the Worlds: Gaming and the Metaverse."

Finally, we look towards the future, combining advances in the capture of movement through to the potential of AI and direct links into the human brain. We re-explore the concept of cities and how should be our future maybe one of living directly in the Metaverse—a concept we term Digital Habitation. It is some time off, but it's coming.

Science fiction has played a pivotal role in shaping the concept of the Metaverse, either through predictive narratives or influential portrayals. From Neal Stephenson's novel Snow Crash, quoted at the beginning of this book, to the Holodeck from Star Trek and Steven Spielberg's 2018 film Ready Player One, these works have presented visions of a future that was once science fiction but are now rapidly becoming science fact. If you have visited before but left as the hype dropped down and worlds became abandoned, then welcome back to the Metaverse. If you are new to the concept, then welcome to the next great frontier of our urban existence.

Before we step forward and examine current systems, avatars and the cities of the Metaverse, it is worth looking back to when the Metaverse was arguably at the peak of its first wave of hype, 1998. Long before the rise of social networks a system known as Active Worlds was pioneering the way forward.

Reference

Gelernter, D. (1991). Mirror worlds: Or: The day software puts the universe in a shoebox ... How it will happen and what it will mean. Oxford University Press.
Gibson, W. (1997). Neuromancer. Penguin Putnam.
Grieves, M. (2015). Digital twin: Manufacturing excellence through virtual factory replication. 3DS. https://www.3ds.com/fileadmin/PRODUCTS-SERVICES/DELMIA/PDF/Whitepaper/DELMIA-APRISO-Digital-Twin-Whitepaper.pdf
Roush, W. (2007, June 18). Second Earth. MIT Technology Review. https://www.technologyreview.com/2007/06/18/272040/second-earth
Stephenson, N. (1992). Snow Crash. Bantam Books.

1

The Early Frontier

Introduction

The early days of the Metaverse were marked by a pioneering spirit, with digital explorers venturing into uncharted virtual realms. In 1998, as the internet was still in its infancy and social media platforms like Facebook (now Meta) and Twitter (now X) were years away, a group of avatars congregated in a three-dimensional world called "Active Worlds." This virtual space, hosted on a modest Windows 95 machine in a research lab at University College London (UCL), became the testing ground for an ambitious experiment: "30 Days in Active Worlds" and one that truly gave an insight into the early frontier of the Metaverse.

The premise was simple—create an open virtual world without rules or restrictions and document what people would build and how a community would form. Led by researchers at UCL's Centre for Advanced Spatial Analysis (CASA), this digital frontier was a blank canvas, a vast expanse of virtual land waiting to be claimed and shaped by its inhabitants.

Over the course of 30 days, a vibrant community emerged, constructing homes, businesses, and even a church, all while forging social connections that transcended physical boundaries. This chapter takes us on a journey through those formative days, to highlight the pioneering spirit of the early Metaverse, capturing the excitement, challenges, and unforeseen consequences of pioneering a new digital realm at the frontier of the Metaverse.

These were the early days of the Metaverse, it really was just emerging as a concept online, there was a feeling of being a pioneer in a new digital world where people appeared as avatars and communicated via typed text. To put 1998 and the then Metaverse into context, it was six years before the introduction of Facebook, seven years before Twitter, and the emerging social networks at that time were taking place in fully three-dimensional worlds inhabited by avatars. These avatars knew they were on the edge of something new, logging in from a personal computer somewhere in the world to not only join in the conversation but also to build, for these worlds were created block by block by the people logging into them. They started as simply empty pieces of land standing like vast fields of grass, with the ability

DOI: 10.1201/9781003440437-1

to add walls, doors, windows, and any number of objects from a database of 3D objects, and ended up as towns and cities of homes and places which thrived. This was the early Metaverse, a compilation of various software systems allowing ways to inhabit and build in three-dimensional space.

At CASA, experiments were conducted with the future of technology. The lab was abuzz with full virtual reality suites, high-end immersive screens, and as part of the buzz, these emerging online spaces, digital worlds living on servers, began to catch the lab's attention. The worlds acted as a series of portals into spaces, enabling you to "teleport" between locations, jumping from world to world with new 3D spaces occupied by people loading on a screen at each jump. It was also possible at that time to set up your own world by simply downloading a "Universe Server," a piece of software which essentially granted you a piece of empty real estate the size of Soho in Central London. With this software installed from a company known as Active Worlds, the idea was born to open up our own world and see if anyone would teleport into it and start building. The aim was to run the world for a month under the title of "30 Days in Active Worlds," the name stemming from the free trial software of the Active Worlds Server which operated for 30 days before timing out. It would turn out to be a long, intriguing month, providing a glimpse into not only what is built but also the social life of the Metaverse.

Within the realm of Metaverses, Active Worlds stands as a notable and enduring presence. Operating on a conventional Windows-based system and headquartered north of Boston, the Active Worlds Universe encompassed a constellation of over 700 distinct worlds, each inhabited by an average of 400 concurrent users. While this figure may seem modest compared to contemporary social networks such as Meta, X, or Tik Tok with their vast user bases, it is essential to consider the context of the era. During Active Worlds' inception, social networks and indeed smartphones were yet to emerge, with the iPhone's introduction still eight years into the future. Users within Active Worlds were not referred to as such but rather as "citizens," reflecting the platform's emphasis on community and spatial engagement. Each citizen possessed an avatar customisable with a range of options, from the burly "Butch" to the feminine "Tanya," along with various intermediate forms. As users typed in their messages, text would appear above their heads, creating the essence of communication within the three-dimensional space.

Within each Metaverse system exists an established set of rules, terms, and conditions to which users must consent upon entering a world. It is the same nowadays with applications on mobile phones; you click "agree" to the terms and conditions and are thus bound to remain within the application rules. The rules of the Metaverse change according to the system and, in certain respects, bear resemblance to theme parks; while visitors are granted entry and permitted to enjoy the space, there are specific actions that are prohibited. As we were running our own server, we decided while talking to a journalist named Tony Durham to deviate slightly and to have a world without any rules or barriers—a world where anything was possible. Tony represented *The Times Higher Education Supplement* (a supplement of the *Times Newspaper*, concentrating on high education) and was inquiring about the laboratory's research endeavours, having familiarised himself with related work discussed in the previous month's edition of the *Sunday Telegraph Magazine* (a *Sunday Newspaper Supplement* in the United Kingdom). Thus, amidst our dialogue, the notion emerged to open our server to the world, granting individuals the freedom to construct, express themselves, and engage in activities as they desired, all in the interest of research (in academic terminology, this endeavour could be classified as a confluence of social science, human-computer interaction, and urban research). All occurrences within this world would be documented, providing insights into what was built, by whom, at what time, and when. In essence, this undertaking would allow us to observe and record the evolution of a virtual world and its associated community from its inception on Day 1 until its planned closure on Day 30.

Preparations were made for the project's launch, set for November 30, 1998, with the *Times Higher Education Supplement* planning to publish an article about the world in the subsequent weeks. Accordingly, we set about creating welcoming signage and an entry space at Ground Zero, located at the coordinates 0 N, 0 W as per the Active Worlds coordinate system. Our world extended outward to 70 N and 70 W, encompassing an area of empty grassland approximately the size of Soho, which was ready to be built upon. The primary feature of Active Worlds, and indeed many subsequent Metaverse systems, is the ability for users to claim land and engage in construction. Building was facilitated through a selection of predefined objects ranging from windows, doors, and walls to trees, shrubs, and paving tiles. These objects could be cloned and strategically placed on the virtual land, essentially resembling an extensive virtual "Lego" set. To assist users within our world, a builder's yard was established at the coordinates 69 N, 69 W, featuring an array of 368 objects. These objects were readily available for selection and cloning, thus initiating the building process.

The process was helped with the layout of the builder's yard by two citizens we had met before in Active Worlds, going by the names of Princess Tia (logging in from New York) and Dawny (logging in from Arizona). Princess Tia and Dawny floated 50 metres above the builder's yard and painstakingly cloned and placed each object in position, ready for the public opening. While they were in the virtual world, a web page was set up to introduce the project, and at the same time, we hooked up our webcam to stream live pictures of the lab into Ground Zero for the opening, to give it more of a personal feel. "30 Days in Active Worlds" was, perhaps unwisely in hindsight, the first Metaverse world to open up without any guidelines or laws. The aim was to see what people would build if they were allowed to build anything they wanted. To check everything was working as expected, we left the server open to the world overnight, two days before the launch, without any rules or regulations in place.

Upon arriving at CASA, located then in the basement of a University building in the Bloomsbury Quarter of London, and logging into the world, we were greeted with two large signs placed by an anonymous user. The first sign had an image linked in from a sex-orientated website, and the second sign was text linking the image with my mother. To say the least, this did not bode well, and with the world set to go live on a University server and the work being covered by the *Times Higher Education Supplement*, we had to tidy up and introduce our first law—no pornographic images. With the first law of "30 Days in Active Worlds" in place, we sat back and waited for the people to come and build, alongside a little bit of trepidation about what would follow over the next month or so.

Day 1

The spatial dimension of the Active Worlds Universe at that particular time was approximately double the expanse of California in the United States. Even in 1998, the Metaverse had achieved a considerable scale; however, its growth was arguably limited primarily by the capacity of the servers that supported its infrastructure. In the case of Active Worlds, this capacity was approximately 800,000 square kilometres. Consequently, despite the significant number of users, the worlds within the Metaverse were sparsely populated, with typically only one or two users per world. Therefore, to attract attention to a particular world and encourage its population growth, thereby increasing the likelihood of documenting the construction of a new Metaverse world, a compelling incentive was necessary. It was widely acknowledged that launching a world without the prospect of users engaging in its development would simply result in an empty plot of land. Given the vastness of the Active Worlds Universe at that time, this outcome was a distinct possibility. An adage posits that "if you build it, they will come," as exemplified in the cinematic production entitled "Field of Dreams." However, this maxim does not appear to hold true in the context of the Metaverse. It is not necessarily the case that simply creating a world will guarantee its success, especially if the onus of construction is placed upon others rather than the creators themselves. Consequently, we determined that organising a building competition would be an effective strategy. To incentivise participation, we offered a prize of one year of complimentary citizenship in Active Worlds to the individual or group that submitted the best design within a 30-day period.

At that time, membership in Active Worlds entailed an annual fee of $19.95, which granted users the ability to engage in construction activities within the virtual worlds. Without membership, individuals were classified as "tourists," which limited their use of avatars and their capacity to secure building plots. The concept of membership in the Metaverse is a common practice, as it provides a revenue stream for the host companies and enables the implementation of various benefits for members, such as the right to place objects within the virtual environment and ensure the security and persistent linkage of those objects to a specific user. However, this approach creates a two-tiered system of citizenship. We aimed to level out this imposed societal structure by actively encouraging tourists to engage with our world. To this end, we permitted tourists to compete for citizenship status, confident in the knowledge that the world was securely logged and backed up every night to mitigate the potential for criminal activity or vandalism (on this one presumption, we were clearly wrong, and we explore this further in Chapter 3 in terms of security and the Metaverse). We achieved a degree of equality by granting both tourists and citizens equal rights in terms of where they could build. However, certain aspects of segregation were "hard coded" into the software. For instance, tourists were limited to a choice of two avatars within the world, in contrast to the standard selection of over twenty avatars available to citizens. This distinction made tourists immediately recognisable as the default "tourist" avatar typically consisted of a male or female figure with a camera around their neck, sunglasses, and other visual elements indicative of a tourist. To address this issue, we custom-designed two avatars that would blend more seamlessly into the overall environment. By eliminating the cameras around their necks and providing them with a more standard appearance, along with the right to build, we aimed to equalise the social dynamics and observe what individuals would create in this frontier.

The launch of the project consisted of Princess Tia and a representative from the lab (Andy, known as Smithee online at the time, a PhD student in the department) standing around at Ground Zero, looking up at the webcam that was plugged in, having a streamed video image of himself which was displayed at 50 feet above the central region. An advert was kindly placed by Active Worlds in AlphaWorld, the most popular of the worlds in the universe, and various messages were sent across newsgroups. AlphaWorld was the centre of the Active Worlds Universe, it was where all users would initially appear upon logging in, at that time it was arguably the centre of the Metaverse. Newsgroups were the alternative best way to reach online citizens at that point in time, as it was before the rise of social networks, and as noted, years before the introduction of Meta—they really were pioneering times.

In real-world terms, having a presence at the entry point of AlphaWorld was like having an advert and live webcam feed beamed into Times Square in New York. Princess Tia acted as a meeter and greeter, showing users around and letting them know they could build anything anywhere. An automatic message also warned them that all conversation and building were logged just to cover any issues of privacy. Dawny logged in from Arizonia in the United States, around 2 pm Greenwich Mean Time, and kindly acted as a representative from the world. She went out around the other worlds, recruiting users to come into "30 Days in Active Worlds" and start building. This began to give the project the momentum it needed and, more importantly, started the word of mouth that would eventually create a complex social world existing in the Windows 95 box in the corner of our small research lab in Central London.

As part of the project's website, a daily news section was set up to document the major events in the world. The site also provided images of the buildings constructed daily and displayed a map of the world so far. On Day 1, 36 registered citizens and an unknown number of tourists placed a total of 6,430 objects in the world. The number of tourists is unknown as they only count as "one" on the builders' list that was used to map the world every 24 hours; we estimated that there were twice as many tourists as there were citizens, a ratio that increased as word spread that we were offering the prize of a free citizenship. The amount of growth was notable; overnight, "30 Days in Active Worlds" became the third most popular world in the Active Worlds Universe and introduced a number of Avatars who would become regular faces over the course of the next 29 remaining days.

The first few days of growth went well, and the research was generating interest from various branches of the media. On Day 2, BBC Radio 4 dropped into Betty B's house, located west of Ground Zero. Betty, logging in from Amsterdam in the Netherlands, had built up a house based on the ideas of cubist design. Although the interior was still basic, it had a path with an American-style mailbox (linked to her Hotmail account) and the beginnings of a well-planted garden. The world began to have a structure—the beginnings of a small settlement, a village in the Metaverse. A technology journalist from the Press Association in the United Kingdom, Lawrence, known as Lorca in Active Worlds, also joined the world to write about the launch and how a new community was being built on the frontier of the Metaverse. Lorca had a deadline to meet, so an interview was carried out at Ground Zero, and he was introduced to Princess Tia and Betty B. Despite a tight deadline, Lorca stayed in the world during the day and even remained after work when his real-world office closed. This was an indication of things to come, as a number of us would spend almost every waking hour in the world—building, talking, and generally exploring what was possible in these new lands for the duration of the project.

Virtual Coffee—Community in 30 Days

The concept of community has been a pivotal factor in the evolution of any Metaverse, dating back to rudimentary text-based systems such as LaMDA MOO (an early text-based Metaverse exclusively based on textual communication) and three-dimensional virtual environments like Active Worlds, leading up to the contemporary systems such as Meta's Horizon, which we explore in the following chapter. The flourishing or decline of a world is primarily determined by the size and enthusiasm of its community. "30 Days in Active Worlds" fell in line with this principle. Thriving environments transform into vibrant, dynamic spaces on the cusp of uncharted territories, while declining worlds often become deserted and desolate places, still present but devoid of inhabitants. We explore this phenomenon further in Chapter 5. Our community had, at this point, positioned itself firmly on the frontier,

FIGURE 1.1
A group of avatars at Ground Zero of "30 Days in Active Worlds."

emerging as a vibrant and expanding group of people building, working, and socialising in this new space.

The "photograph" in Figure 1.1 was taken half way through the experiment, marking the establishment of a close-knit community. While the names of those depicted are not easily discernible, they can be identified based on their physical attributes, much like in real life. Dawny, a resident of Arizona, United States, embraced the "Tanya" avatar, characterised by long, flowing red hair and a green dress reminiscent of the 1970s. In contrast, Betty B, hailing from Amsterdam, opted for the "Rachel" avatar, featuring blonde hair tied in a ponytail. Lorca, a journalist who had dedicated himself almost entirely to "30 Days" in Active Worlds, consistently used the "James" avatar. Stick, a resident of Bristol in the United Kingdom, chose the "Hotep" avatar, navigating the world in Egyptian attire. The participants had a selection of over 20 avatars, each distinct in appearance and closely resembling their personal identities within the Metaverse. At that time, each system maintained its own set of avatars, resulting in different identities for users in each Metaverse. It is only now that standardised protocols are gradually emerging, allowing users to carry their avatars across different virtual worlds.

Avatars become associated with a person and, in a sense, each avatar begins to resemble a friendly face when either entering the world or walking in on one of the social gatherings that took place. The exception to each person's use of a fixed avatar was National Butch Day, organised by Stick. Stick organised the day via a series of emails and telegrams, informing users that they were required to adopt the Butch Avatar for the duration of Day 20. Butch was selected because he was Andy's avatar identity in the world. Andy was blissfully unaware of the nature of the day until he logged in as usual and found a group of users around Ground Zero all looking like him with the Butch avatar! His initial confusion, not having recognisable faces to identify, was greeted with much amusement and provided the opportunity for numerous Smithee (Andy's online username) impersonations by the community members.

These occurrences serve to highlight the development of a profound sense of community. Consistent with numerous descriptions of the Metaverse, readers often gain the impression that physical presence was essential for fully grasping the depth of involvement. The phrase "Being There" aptly captures the prevailing sentiment of community engagement and excitement. Participants felt as though they were partaking in an endeavour with the potential to shape the history of virtual worlds and communities. A pioneering spirit emerged, characterised by the drive to mould new worlds and explore possibilities. Logging into the virtual environment became akin to returning home. Each day, Andy would depart from his compact abode in North London, board the underground railway to Kings Cross Station, arrive at his workplace, and proceed to log in. Upon his avatar's appearance at Ground Zero, he would be warmly greeted by users who had already logged in. These individuals would extend cordial greetings of good morning, afternoon, or evening, reflecting their real-world time zones. The daily routine consisted of examining newly constructed buildings and engaging in virtual discussions over virtual coffee, aiming to find solutions to various challenges.

During the login process, many individuals experienced a profound sense of familiarity akin to being at home. An increasing number of users became immersed in this novel virtual realm to the extent that, as the Christmas period drew near, a Christmas tree adorned with sparkling lights and surrounded by presents was planted at Ground Zero. On Christmas Day, shortly after partaking in his real-world Christmas lunch, Andy notes that, he felt an irresistible pull towards the Metaverse. Consequently, he discreetly left his family's Christmas celebration and accessed his laptop. To his surprise, he discovered several other users online, and he spontaneously decided to hold an impromptu carol service around the virtual Christmas tree. They gathered together and linked some MIDI-based music to the virtual world, enabling them to listen to carols. The first carol chosen was "O Come All Ye Faithful," which they subsequently "sang" or more accurately typed. It was a surreal experience to be "typing carols" with individuals from around the globe on Christmas Day in the Metaverse. Upon discovering that he had logged on and engaged in this virtual carolling, Andy's family expressed mild concern. They questioned why he had opted to enter a virtual realm filled with digital carols and presents instead of watching the traditional then Queen's Speech. While their perspective had merit, it is essential to recognise that the Metaverse offers a unique and immersive experience, akin to discovering a new place or home, which captivated Andys attention and drew him in.

The webcam, which served to transmit visual representations of Andy and the computer upon which the virtual world was maintained, was in a state of continuous operation. Over time, he developed a propensity to disregard its presence entirely. Its primary objective was to provide a human dimension to the virtual world, thereby ensuring that users were aware of the human agency behind its operation. In some respects, it may have evoked a sense of illusion akin to the Wizard of Oz, looking over the world. However, its sole purpose was to establish a connection between the tangible and the intangible realms. The webcam's presence was acknowledged by the participants of the virtual world, and as early as the second day, screenshots derived from the webcam were being disseminated on a global scale. One notable incident involved replicating the live webcam feed onto four sides of a cube, which was subsequently placed atop a towering column overlooking the virtual world. Encircling the column were depictions of avatars, their hands raised in a gesture of reverence towards his image. This arrangement imparted an almost divine aura to the webcam, with Andy's likeness gazing upon the world he had fashioned. In the ensuing weeks, the webcam became a focal point for certain members of the community.

One anonymous member (henceforth referred to as "James") connected on the 12th day and inquired if Andy would visit and inspect his newly constructed virtual home. Given the central importance of buildings to the world's nature, such requests were customary. However, he was entirely unprepared for what awaited upon entering his virtual abode. Entering his virtual lounging area, the walls were adorned with numerous images of Andy. These images were captured from the webcam and stored on an external web server, facilitating hotlinking back into the virtual world. The images depicted his typical office routine, which, arguably, lacked much inherent interest. Several images depicted Andy holding a cup of coffee, another holding a chocolate bar, and others depicted him seated while consuming his lunch. Each image was accompanied by a caption such as "Smithee enjoys coffee" or, in the case of an image of a vacant chair, "Where is our leader?" When James inquired about his opinion on his new virtual home, Andy found himself momentarily speechless. The question that occupied his mind was "Why?" In this uncharted territory, why would the connection to the real world accorded such significance? It then dawned on him that while he was examining the virtual home and the images of Andy, he was also being observed live via the webcam. James inquired about Andy's evident shock, to which he attributed it to an email he had been reading rather than the presence of images depicting his real-world self throughout his virtual lounge.

Following the discovery of the images in James's virtual lounge, Andy experienced a persistent sensation of being watched. In retrospect, this reaction appears ludicrous, as such surveillance is inherent to the purpose of a webcam; however, at the time, he had subconsciously relegated it to a background element of the project. Nevertheless, he resolved to temporarily disable the webcam for a few days, attributing the blank screens to a technical error. During his absence from the office, one of our colleagues received a phone call from James, who requested that he reconnect the webcam without informing Andy, thereby enabling continued observation upon his return. The colleague declined the request and informed Andy about the incident. It became apparent that he had inadvertently exposed himself to the online world. His telephone number and location were publicly accessible on our primary research website, and live images were being broadcast globally. While the intention behind these actions was to ground the research and humanise it, it somehow perceived a boundary violation between the virtual world that he had created and the real world in which he was, arguably, working.

Andy connected to the virtual world and initiated a conversation with James. Reservations were expressed regarding the reactivation of the webcam via a phone call to the office, emphasising the belief that virtual and real domains ought to remain distinct. James did not appear to share the concerns, but somehow there was an intuitive sense that a boundary had been crossed. The webcam had evolved into a distraction from the world's intended purpose rather than enhancing it. As a result, the webcam remained offline for the remainder of the "30 Days in Active Worlds" experiment. In retrospect, it could have potentially been left enabled, but at the time, streaming services and platforms like YouTube, where individuals actively stream live content, were not yet commonplace. In those early days, a tangible divide still existed between the real and virtual realms.

The Start of a Town

In the virtual worlds of the Metaverse, the development of cities transpires gradually, unless they are engineered by artificial intelligence, a concept which we will explore later in Chapter 6. As opposed to the real world, the process of constructing elements such as walls and doors is slow in the Metaverse, yet by the end of the 30th day, the virtual world had been adorned with over 27,699 objects meticulously placed by 49 registered users and an unspecified number of transient visitors.

Figure 1.2 depicts the final map of the world, highlighting its structures and infrastructure. The map adopts a top-down "satellite" perspective, distinct from the view typically observed by users of the world. This vantage point facilitates the visualisation of its spatial arrangement. The world comprised various structures, including residential streets, nightclubs, museums, bars, healthcare facilities, and even a lovers' lane supplemented by an adjoining motel. Many of these structures mirrored real-world counterparts, serving as early digital twins within the Metaverse. Country cottages were prevalent, characterised by extensive tree-lined pathways leading to rustic front doors and culminating in open spaces with roaring fireplaces. Notably, wooden American-style lodges stood side-by-side with towering glass skyscrapers and ethereal floating castles. In terms of spatial organisation, the project intentionally lacked a defined structure, consistent with its overarching plan. Notably, there was no designated downtown or central hub (apart from the entry point), reflecting a more organic approach emphasising land acquisition and the gradual formation of a community. In their subsequent

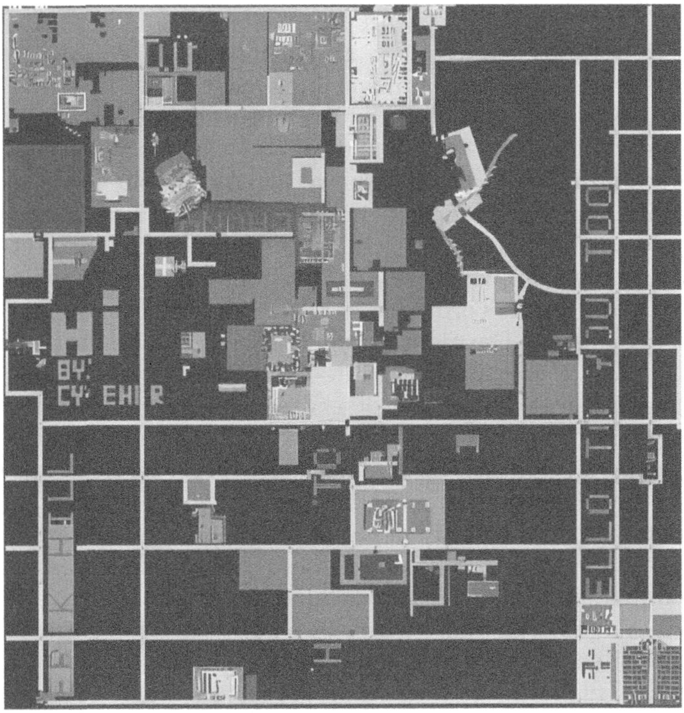

FIGURE 1.2
Map of the final days building in "30 Days in Active Worlds."

analysis of the project, Schroeder et al. (2001) observed that the early structures in Active Worlds resembled log cabins, bearing a closer resemblance to the television series "Little House on the Prairie" than to the anticipated "cyberspace." This observation arguably highlights the project's alignment with a frontier-like philosophy.

During the 30-day period of the Active Worlds experiment, participants engaged in the construction of a virtual environment using a predetermined set of objects. In addition to the inherent characteristics of these objects, there was a prevailing tendency among users to create structures that closely mirrored the real world within the constraints of the system. One notable example of this was the construction of a bar within the virtual world, complete with a toilet featuring urinals, washbasins, and a mirror. While these objects served no obvious or functional purpose, they contributed to the immersive experience within the world. Similarly, a grid-pattern road layout was implemented throughout the world (by Andy, Betty B, and Dawny), with the intent of influencing its development and extending its reach along the newly placed highways. This endeavour required substantial manual labour, particularly considering the absence of cars or vehicles within Active Worlds. It is worth noting that cars were a relatively recent addition to virtual worlds, with their most prominent implementation being in Spatial.io, which will be explored later. One of the motivations behind the construction efforts was the knowledge that the world was mapped every 24 hours, with the resulting image being displayed on the website's news page. The prospect of seeing one's creations immortalised on the map led to a wave of "satellite writing"—text that, while indistinguishable from the ground, would become visible when the world was mapped from above, akin to the Nazca Lines in the Peruvian Desert which are only discernible from an aerial perspective. The nightly mapping process, with the finalised outcome in Figure 1.2, provided a satellite-like view of the world as it evolved, revealing structures that would otherwise remain hidden from ground-level observation. The first words to appear on the map were "Hi" on Day 6, followed by the addition of "By Cyberhar" on Day 7. Cyberhar was also responsible for the construction of the CyberHar Castle and an Alien made of coloured glass in the northern regions of the world.

Lover's Lane was a unique creation within the virtual world, engaging the entire community. Initiated by Dawny and her real-life partner Ken, it was conceived as a romantic space where love poems and photographs of partners could be shared. Through the community's contributions, it evolved into a broader platform, showcasing photographs not only of romantic partners but also of individuals in general. It became a focal point for members of the "30 Days" community to connect and learn about each other. The photographs even extended to include images of pets, family, and friends, humanising the virtual world. Lover's Lane exemplified a community-built space for the benefit of its members, while Stick pursued a separate construction project geared towards an external community. Stick's Community Church, constructed within "30 Days," served the specific purpose of facilitating prayer.

The Church, designed in a Victorian-style English Christian architecture, featured a bell tower, stained glass windows, and a church organ. While built within the "30 Days" environment, its intended purpose extended beyond the internal community. Instead, it catered to the youth section of the Alpha Church, based in Brompton, London, particularly the Sunday School section. The church's name "Alpha" and its proximity to Alpha World were coincidental but seamlessly integrated it within the Active Worlds Universe. Actively utilised for meetings, it stands as the sole structure within the virtual world that served a purpose beyond the digital realm.

It is noteworthy that although a church within "30 Days" might initially appear incapable of replicating real-world church services, its existence signifies the community's maturation. Virtual churches are prevalent in numerous virtual world communities and tend to emerge as the community matures. While Andy did not personally attend any services held in

"30 Days," he did find it reassuring to witness certain sections of the virtual world being utilised for such purposes.

"30 Days II" and Beyond

From the initial launch, the anticipated fate of the world following the "30 Days" event was clearly communicated on the web page: it was projected to be on the trajectory of an incoming asteroid and consequently would be annihilated. In actuality, the sole repercussion would have been the resetting of the server adjacent to our desks, subsequently enabling the world to be repurposed for alternative research pursuits. Nevertheless, as the "30 Days" event drew to a close, community members unequivocally expressed their desire for the preservation of the world and its community intact. Owing to its successful capture of media attention, the organisation responsible for Active Worlds kindly granted a complimentary one-year license for the server, thus facilitating the continued operation of the world. This extension of the world's existence was marked by the launch of "30 Days II," which entailed a paradigm shift: instead of relying solely on the existing object set, users were empowered to design and incorporate their own custom objects into the world. A dedicated website was developed and linked to various 3D software packages, along with comprehensive documentation on the intricacies of object creation for Active Worlds, a task acknowledged as being inherently challenging. Furthermore, a novel incentive was introduced in the form of a CD-ROM version of Active Worlds valued at $50, which offered the capability for high-resolution textures. Additionally, ongoing efforts were undertaken to map and log the world.

Only a limited number of custom objects were submitted, namely: a Condom Machine (intended for placement near Lover's Lane), a Moon, a Park Bench, and a Carousel. The scarcity of objects serves as a testament to the inherent difficulties associated with creating custom content for the Metaverse. This is something we explore further in Chapter 4, especially around open-source 3D modelling software such as Blender. Consequently, the majority of users opted to continue utilising the standard object set provided by the Builder's Yard. During the midpoint of "30 Days II," a significant change occurred in Andys' work circumstances as he moved to a new employment contract. While he maintained his commitment to mapping the world, the demands of the new role precluded him from dedicating eight hours per day to the task, as had been the case during the preceding "30 Days" event. Consequently, the number of users frequenting the world began to dwindle, eventually resulting in a peak population of merely two to –three users. It was becoming a deserted world, a phenomenon which is all too common in the Metaverse, something we explore in more detail in Chapter 5.

Within the vast expanse of the Active Worlds Universe, a palpable aura of emptiness and abandonment descended upon the world, rendering it akin to a forsaken ghost town. This pervasive atmosphere of desolation was not confined to a single location but rather permeated the diverse regions of the Metaverse. The genesis of this "ghost town" effect can be traced back to the frontier philosophy embedded within the very fabric of the Metaverse. In nascent virtual worlds, population levels tend to experience a surge as individuals are captivated by the allure of participating in a novel and uncharted endeavour. However, as these worlds mature and the finite land resources become increasingly claimed, a significant portion of the population embarks on a migratory journey in search of unexplored territories, leaving behind a desolate and forsaken virtual landscape in their wake.

"30 Days in Active Worlds" experienced a boom—a period of rapid development initially with the creation of physical structures and then with the formation of a vibrant community. As users constructed virtual homes, nightclubs, and other structures, the world became a popular gathering place for socialising, which led to a decline in the pace of construction. A unique feature of 30 Days was its 30-day logging and mapping period, with a prize offered at the conclusion. Despite the community's initial aspiration to sustain the world, members eventually migrated to other platforms, particularly Second Life, which we explore more of later, and other multi-user systems. One such user, Stick, continued to visit the Church for a year before his Active Worlds membership expired. Another user, Lorca, resumed his journalistic pursuits, catching up on the work he had neglected while immersed in the experiment. A remarkable encounter occurred ten years later at the National Maritime Museum in London, where the Andy and Lorca met in person by accident in a meeting, an extraordinary experience considering their previous interactions had been confined to the Metaverse. Lorca looks different from his avatar.... But then again so does Andy.

In another twist to the tale, in the period prior to the closure of the world, Dawny and Ken had formulated plans to marry, and they wanted to get married in the virtual world. This event was intended to mark the inaugural reunion of "30 Days," with Stick undertaking the role of Virtual Vicar and presiding over the reopening of the church. It would have been the world's first wedding in the Metaverse. However, a sequence of unforeseen circumstances regrettably prevented the wedding from taking place. Dawny and Ken experienced a separation shortly before the scheduled nuptials, and tragically, Ken succumbed to a cardiac event and died in real life. Subsequently, Dawny reached out, expressing her desire to revisit "30 Days in Active Worlds" and view the structures Ken had constructed in Lover's Lane.

As such, rather than hold a Wedding, we held the first Funeral in the Metaverse at the Church. In a sombre gesture, a period of silence was observed throughout the world, followed by a service for Ken. His avatar was rotated 90 degrees and interred underground in close proximity to the church. Although not the first wedding, this event marking the first funeral in the Metaverse seemed somehow a fitting send-off that resonated deeply within the community. After the funeral, other users embarked upon the creation of their own worlds within the Active Worlds Universe. Reflecting on the time spent in "30 Days in Active Worlds," Andy resolved to venture back into the physical world. However, the allure of the Metaverse proved irresistible, and it was not long before his avatar "Smithee" emerged in other systems—Second Life, Meta's Horizon, Spatial.io, and several other platforms that we explore in greater depth in the following chapters.

In evaluating the impact of "30 Days," it stands as the first world to be fully mapped and logged. The maps have been featured in various publications dedicated to the history of virtual worlds. It represented an early frontier space and offered a glimpse into what we now recognise as the Metaverse. This digital realm facilitated shared experiences, enabling users to engage with one another and the virtual environment. The Metaverse, in its evolving state, holds the potential to encompass diverse aspects of our online lives, ranging from social interactions to work, entertainment, and commercial transactions. Notably, "30 Days" fostered the development of a thriving community within a small desktop computer in the basement of a research lab in Central London, underscoring the profound impact that virtual worlds can have on human connections and perhaps providing a glimpse of the future of the Metaverse.

Reference

Schroeder, R., Huxor, A., & Hudson-Smith, A. (2001). Activeworlds: Geography and social interaction in virtual reality. Futures, 33(7), 569–587. 10.1016/S0016-3287(01)00002-7.

2

The Metascape: Cities and Avatars

Introduction

The urban landscapes of the Metaverse represent a stark departure from the well-defined structures and layouts of traditional cities. Unbound by geographical boundaries, physical resources, or conventional architectural paradigms, these virtual cities transcend the constraints of the physical world. They manifest as sprawling, interconnected spaces where imagination and creativity reign supreme, giving rise to environments that mirror utopian ideals or serve as cautionary tales of dystopian futures.

At the heart of these digital realms lie avatars—our virtual manifestations that traverse and shape these landscapes. No longer limited to static representations, avatars are evolving to reflect the nuances of human behaviour, emotions, and personality traits. They are becoming extensions of our physical selves, capable of mirroring our movements, facial expressions, and even vocal patterns, blurring the boundaries between the tangible and the virtual.

The Metaverse is not a monolithic entity but is arguably a tapestry woven from the collective efforts of millions of individuals and entities worldwide—creating a metascape. From gaming platforms at the edge of the Metaverse like Roblox and Fortnite (which we explore more of in Chapter 4) to dedicated Metaverse environments like Decentraland and Meta Horizons, each digital realm contributes its unique thread to the metascape. Akin to the cities of the physical world, these virtual spaces host a vibrant array of commerce, social interaction, and entertainment, fostering communities that transcend geographical limitations.

At the intersection of the Metaverse and the physical world lies the concept of digital twins—virtual replicas that mirror their real-world counterparts, augmented with data streams and interactive elements. These twins serve as gateways, allowing seamless transitions between the tangible and the digital, blending realities in ways that were once confined to the realms of science fiction.

In this chapter, we delve into the intricate landscapes of the Metaverse, exploring the dynamic nature of its cities, the evolution of avatars, and the convergence of physical and virtual spaces. We unravel the threads that

DOI: 10.1201/9781003440437-2

weave together this tapestry, shedding light on the pioneers, innovators, and visionaries who are shaping the urban environments of tomorrow, one digital brick at a time.

These digital cities exude dynamism, interactivity, and fluidity, encapsulating a vast array of possibilities and experiences that are continuously shaped and reshaped by the collective and individual actions of their digital inhabitants.

Current Metaverse Systems

At the time of writing, there were over 170 companies building the Metaverse, a term which arguably implies one singular space but, in reality, relates to the many coexisting Metaverses under development. As we have explored in the introduction, the term Metaverse is relatively new, the concept arguably emerging from Stephenson's (1992, p. 35) vision in his novel "Snow Crash" where he first describes the Metaverse:

> *As Hiro approaches the Street, he sees two young couples, probably using their parents' computer for a double date in the Metaverse, climbing down out of Port Zero, which is the local port of entry and monorail stop. He is not seeing real people, of course. This is all part of the moving illustration drawn by his computer according to the specifications coming down the fibre-optic cable. The people are pieces of software called avatars.*

Although this is the first use of the term, taking a step back from Stephenson's concept of The Street and Port Zero, the Metaverse can be viewed as a digital space, often with an economic structure and occupied by avatars, sometimes mirroring the real world but with multiple representations of the physical world and the ability to change time, physics, and space. Stephenson's vision is undoubtedly urban; it is a cityscape existing in the illustration downloaded by the fibre-optic cable.

The illustration of the city is in reality, layers of digital information. Building and adapting from Radoff (2021), these Metaverse layers to form cityscapes rely on distinct aspects:

1. Infrastructure: Connectivity technologies like 5G, Wi-Fi, cloud, and Stephenson's fibre-optic cable. Indeed, the move of fibre direct to homes in terms of internet provider technology is only now becoming more common, allowing faster access to data and, with it, the ability to download, or stream, larger and more complex worlds.
2. Human Interface: Virtual reality (VR) headsets, augmented reality (AR) glasses, haptics, and other technologies allow us to join the Metaverse in increasingly immersive ways. The most common are the Quest range of VR Headset from Meta (formerly Facebook) and the Vision Pro from Apple. However, these are not required to enter the Metaverse, only to see it in three dimensions. Most systems also

offer the ability to run on standard laptops on Windows, Linux, or Mac-based machines.

3. Decentralisation: Blockchain, artificial intelligence, edge computing, and other democratisation tools. We move onto these systems in the next chapter and explain blockchain. In essence, they form the underlying financial backbone of the city in the Metaverse, where everything from land to digital assets can be bought and sold, creating a working economy.
4. Spatial Computing: 3D visualisation and modelling frameworks. This is the heart of the system, the ability to render views to create the illustration of place and space. This crosses boundaries from the Metaverse and into actual space, mixing realities and allowing digital assets to appear as if they exist in the real world. Spatial computing allows our real-world homes, neighbourhoods, and cities to become augmented with additional information, like an extension of our laptops, phones, and tablets, but with information existing in our physical spaces.
5. Experiences: Metaverse equivalents of locations and events such as places for work, offices, meeting rooms, and conference locations through to leisure such as multiplex cinemas, concert venues, gaming, and shopping. All of these exist in the Metaverse.

The Metaverse is a complex and multifaceted concept, encompassing a range of layers and dimensions which can collectively be seen as a boundless virtual sandbox for the development of cities. This rapidly evolving field is characterised by the integration of multiple systems and technologies, enabling the creation of immersive digital environments and the seamless interplay of digital assets, particularly avatars. Notably, the announcement from Facebook in September 2021, signalling a $50 million investment in a global research programme dedicated to developing the Metaverse, marked a significant milestone in its evolution. Furthermore, in October 2021, Facebook underwent a rebranding, changing its name to Meta. Andrew Bosworth, the then Vice President of Facebook Reality Labs, outlined a timeline of 10–15 years for the realisation of their vision of the Metaverse, defining it as a virtual space where individuals can engage in creative endeavours and immersive experiences with others who are not physically present in the same location. While platforms such as Active Worlds and others like Second Life have existed since the mid-1990s, many other systems have either ceased operations or remain largely inactive. Chapter 5 of this book further explores the concept of abandoned worlds. Of the numerous Metaverses currently in development, of which there are approximately 170, several key players have emerged, including Meta, Spatial.io, Oncyber.io, and Decentraland. Additionally, three platforms straddle the boundary between Metaverses and gaming worlds: Minecraft, Fortnite, and Roblox. In between these major players, numerous other Metaverses exist, each containing various forms of digital settlements. As such, the landscape of the Metaverse is complex;

within this complexity, many of these Metaverses coalesce into hamlets, villages, towns, and ultimately cities.

Within the Metaverse, the conceptualisation and construction of cities deviate substantially from physical urban spaces. They are not restricted by geographical boundaries, physical resources, or conventional architectural paradigms. Buildings can transcend gravitational constraints, parks can levitate, and streets can distort the fabric of space and time. This results in a realm where the normative principles of urban planning are replaced by imagination and creativity. Such digital freedom facilitates the construction of cities that mirror utopian ideals or serve as dystopian warnings, thereby encompassing the vast spectrum of human aspirations and apprehensions. These cities also function as platforms for cultural, economic, and political interactions, echoing the intricacies and complexities of their real-world counterparts, which is where the concept of digital twins comes in.

Digital Twins

Despite the lack of any geographical, physical, or architectural constraints, there is a trend to simply mirror the real world, creating, in essence, a digital twin—a digital representation of the physical world, often with the addition of data collected from anything from building systems through to social and environmental feeds that can be viewed within the digital space. These twins are in their infancy; the concept is aimed at looking at a mirror of our world, a mirror that not only reflects the environment but also displays the invisible: the flows of data. These, of course, are represented on a display, currently the most common being the computer screen or tablet. However, as we have noted, screens are changing. Systems such as VR, and perhaps with even more potential, mixed reality and the wider concept of spatial computing, will allow us to see these mirror worlds within our actual environment or as a model city with data overlaid. At different scales, data and reality can be mixed, viewed, and shared. Given the pace of technology, the creation of fully functioning digital twins of our current cities and towns is inevitable. London, New York, Paris, Munich—indeed all global cities—will have digital twins, mirroring the world but existing in the Metaverse. There are already government-level plans for these cities. A recent report, "Data for the Public Good," by the UK's National Infrastructure Commission (NIC) proposed the creation of a digital twin to unify the management of data concerning transport, rail, power, water, and communications infrastructures alongside meteorology and demographics across the whole of the United Kingdom. These twins can live either inside or outside of the Metaverse; when they are introduced to a collaborative digital system, they become more than a twin for the management of assets; they become occupied by inhabitants—avatars mixing and interacting not only with the mirror of the models but also the data.

One example to share is ViLO from our research lab—ViLO, short for Virtual London, is an ongoing project aimed at exploring, building, linking, and porting digital twins into the Metaverse (Figure 2.1).

FIGURE 2.1
ViLO–The Virtual London Digital Twin City Model. Credit Authors.

ViLO is presently centred around the Queen Elizabeth Park region of London, which hosted the 2012 Olympic Games. The region offers a valuable testing ground due to its quickly changing landscape and the abundance of accessible data feeds. Currently, at the local level, we can display the real-time movement of the tube, overland trains, and buses; the number of bicycles available for rent at docking stations; live weather feeds ranging from wind speed to ultraviolet levels and temperature; and air quality measurements. At the building level, data accessibility determines the availability of information, as most buildings do not presently share data such as occupancy, energy consumption, and carbon footprint. However, our laboratory has established an offshoot at our new campus UCL East at Queen Elizabeth Park, where we are currently sharing over 10 million data points a day. This enables us to incorporate these points into our model, the Metaverse, and progress towards the creation of a genuine digital twin or mirror world. To make these models occupied, they need to be linked to Metaverse systems and thus populated with avatars, arguably the most important part of the Metaverse.

Avatars

At the human level, digital twins extend to avatars and the ability to create a digital clone of ourselves. Many Metaverse systems come with a predefined choice of standard avatars to use within their system. Avatars therefore differ from system to system, from human to animal through to fantasy realms it is possible to take a myriad of forms. The avatars pictured in Figure 2.2, in our ViLO model are from an open-source system known as Ubiq, are an example of floating avatars, in the Metaverse you do not always have or indeed need legs.

While in most systems avatars can often be configured for hair type, glasses, clothing, etc., it does mean that you often need to design a new avatar whenever you newly log into each system. There are, however, developments to allow avatars to be interchangeable between worlds so your avatar—your identity in the Metaverse—travels with you. It is surprisingly easy to create a digital twin of yourself for an avatar using mobile applications. There are various 3D capture applications; at the time of writing, PolyCam, Magiscan, and In3D are good choices which allow you to pan around yourself with your phone's camera to create a photorealistic 3D model. This model is then automatically augmented with a joint system to simulate your bones and thus allow movement, and within a few minutes, you can find your own digital twin occupying and walking around the Metaverse.

However, at the moment, uploading your digital twin self for use across the Metaverse is still challenging, and third-party companies are emerging

FIGURE 2.2
ViLO populated with avatars from Ubiq.

to try to bridge the gap between your online digital self and the myriad of worlds that make up the Metaverse. One of these is Ready Player Me (a take on the film title "Ready Player One")—they note that at the moment, the future of digital experiences is not a single app. It is a network of millions of virtual worlds and digital experiences people visit to play games, socialise, and collaborate. Today, most of those experiences are closed and disconnected, walled gardens. Ready Player Me is a cross-game avatar platform for developers, creators, and players on a mission to break down the virtual walls to enable more open and connected worlds and any digital experience.

The system allows you to take one of two routes—a photorealistic capture of your face/head via the uploading of a photograph or a more standard, although highly customisable, cartoon-like avatar. Once created, it can be edited at any time to add clothing items (often from brand names which can then be purchased; we explore this concept more in Chapter 3 around the economics of the Metaverse). Arguably, your digital representation in the Metaverse is an extension of your physical self. Although it can take any form, people do tend to get attached to their digital selves. Personally, we have had numerous avatars across many digital worlds, as systems such as Ready Player Me are a new innovation—almost as an evolving stand in of our digital selves. On quite a few of them, one of us (Andy) has spent more on a virtual haircut than he has in real life, and there perhaps lies a lesson for us all. That said, the rise of digital capture technology is making it easy to rapidly capture ourselves and people. As a test, we asked Trevor, a member

FIGURE 2.3
Trevor being digitally scanned. Credit Authors.

of the village where Andy lives to pose to see how quickly we could "import" him into the Metaverse (Figure 2.3).

Using a 3D capture app (Magiscan3D), we were able to take photos of Trevor all the way around while he held out his arms. This allowed us to then overlay a "digital skeleton" on top of his now digital body, allowing us to add movement and the ability to walk. Within 30 minutes, we had a digital twin of Trevor in Spatial.io and by adding predefined animation sets to his new digital bone structure we added to him the ability to dance the Samba. After all if you are going to add someone into the Metaverse you might as well upskill them as well. Sadly, the terms and conditions of the Spatial.io platform does not allow the publication of screenshots (we did ask politely) so we are unable to show you Trevor doing the Samba but you can visit him directly in our world: https://tinyurl.com/yc5cda97. If we are about, do come and say hello.

The use of a twin of our digital selves opens up many ethical and psychological questions about the use of such technology. What if other people started capturing ourselves and using our bodies in the Metaverse? What happens to our digital twins after our death? Despite these and many other emerging questions, our avatars are getting more photorealistic along with the ability to add in lip-syncing and body movements direct from our own hand and face movements.

Whether your choice is to be in pure cartoon form, a digital twin, or somewhere in between, there is now the possibility to move your avatar between worlds. That marks the start of the ability to start occupying not just one Metaverse but the multiverse—a universe of Metaverses.

Twinning Movement

The increasing sophistication of avatars is leading to more nuanced representations of humans, encompassing not only visual appearance but also vocal attributes, body language, and facial expressions. This ability, termed "twin movement," represents a significant advancement in the perception, communication, and experience of the Metaverse. Avatars are transitioning from relatively static representations, observed in platforms like Active Worlds, to manifestations capable of reflecting emotions, intentions, and personality traits. This enhanced realism fosters a deeper sense of connection and presence, bridging the gap between physical and virtual selves.

Among the most fundamental twinning elements, voice communication has become the norm in the Metaverse. In the contemporary context, video conferencing platforms such as Zoom and Teams have made online conversations commonplace. However, in the realm of the Metaverse, voice communication was an innovation introduced back in 1997 with the launch of Onlive Traveller, which enabled users to engage in verbal interaction (Figure 2.4).

Communication within Onlive necessitated the user simultaneously pressing the "ctrl" key on the keyboard and speaking into a microphone. The users' voices were then subjected to encoding before their transmission into

FIGURE 2.4
Onlive Traveller—the first Metaverse with voice communications. Credit Authors.

the virtual environment. This process utilised automated voice synthesis and three-dimensional audio for its implementation. The end result was real-time conversations between lip-synchronised avatars. However, the emphasis on lip synchronisation resulted in the portrayal of the avatars as individual disembodied heads. While this approach provided a novel experience, it inherently limited the level of perceived interaction with the environment. There was no compelling need to develop intricate worlds that included houses, for instance, as the disembodied heads would be unable to navigate through doorways. It is important to note that Onlive was an experimental system, and the audio quality was often inadequate, leading to interruptions and misunderstandings during conversations. In fact, the expressions "pardon" and "what" when uttered in three-dimensional audio were among the most frequently used phrases in Onlive.

In the modern technological landscape, voice communication has become a standard feature, but there are still significant limitations in terms of accurately capturing and replicating physical movements in virtual environments. These limitations manifest in two distinct scales: facial tracking and full-body tracking. Facial expression tracking is primarily confined to Metaverse systems that utilise VR headsets. A notable example is Meta Horizon with Quest Pro and Apple's Vision Pro, which have both experimental "facial expressions" features. They both aim to enhance the naturalness of avatar expressions in virtual environments by detecting facial movements through real-time images and mirroring them in three-dimensional space. The headsets employ image analysis (although both in different ways) to estimate key parameters such as the direction of gaze and facial movements, which are then translated into numerical data. These data points allow for the generation of realistic facial expressions in virtual environments.

VR headsets are in reality an array of sensors, from inward-facing cameras looking at your face and your eyes, to external-facing sensors to understand your environment in three-dimensional space. These outward-facing cameras are able to pick up hand movements, not only the location of your hand but also the movements of your fingers. Apple's version of the avatar is known as a Spatial Persona. Apple has gone down the photorealistic route, using the sensors built into the Vision Pro to provide full lip-syncing and hand movements within the spatial environment. Of note, however, is the distinct lack of anything else from the neck down. In Apple's world, you are a floating head, a little like the concept from Onlive back in the 1990s.

The combination of hand tracking and facial expressions is now allowing avatars to convey, in near real time, your hand, eye, and facial movements to others in the Metaverse. By way of example, Horizons Workrooms (from Meta) is a collaborative space where emotions are actually conveyed by the avatars from the gesture of a hand to a raised eyebrow. This represents a shift in the Metaverse, whereas before you could sit "behind" your avatar, it will now mirror every frown, blink of an eye, or scratch of your head; non-verbal communications have now moved into the digital space.

In the realm of Meta's Horizon, avatars have only recently acquired the ability to possess legs. At its inception, avatars were depicted from the waist up, suspended in mid-air. This design choice was influenced by two primary factors. Firstly, there was the inherent challenge associated with full-body motion tracking. Secondly, individuals engaging in the Metaverse are frequently seated in real life. Consequently, tracking leg movements only became meaningful when sufficient space was available for ambulatory activities. Generally, full-body motion tracking has been confined to the high-end market segments of gaming and motion capture for films and devices where recorded movements are replayed by characters rather than communicated in real time. However, this paradigm has shifted with the recent introduction of Sony's Compact Full Body Motion Capture System, commonly referred to as MoCopi. Comprising six magnetic trackers strategically positioned on the ankles, hips, wrists, and head, MoCopi enables real-time twinning of our body structure.

The system only works in VRChat, another leading Metaverse system which is well worth exploring, it allows avatars to be fully synced with body movements; couple this with facial and hand tracking, and we are moving towards a full twinning of our body movements.

Cities in the Metaverse

Beyond the mix of emerging digital twins, cities in the Metaverse are dynamic entities. They change and evolve, shaped by the actions, interactions, and decisions of their digital inhabitants and visitors. This real-time adaptation creates a sense of living, breathing urban environments that continually respond and adapt to the needs and desires of the community. These cities host a unique mix of commerce, social interaction, and entertainment—analogous to real-world cities. Businesses are able to create virtual storefronts that offer interactive and immersive shopping experiences. Parks and squares become venues for virtual concerts, art exhibits, or community gatherings, fostering social interaction and shared experiences. They are ultimately (currently) shaped by their users (all this is about to change if you jump to Chapter 6 and Turing's Dream), but for the most part to date, the Metaverse has been built and shaped by people. Linking back to "30 Days in Active Worlds," its host world was known as AlphaWorld and it's a key example of the shape of the Metaverse.

As of August 2000, AlphaWorld was made up of 58.5 million objects, each cloned and placed, creating a unique digital geography. The geography of Active Worlds can be traced back to 28 June 1995 when the first Active Worlds server, AlphaWorld, was opened to the internet. Its physical geography was relatively simple: a vast flat plain of virtual land 429,038 × 429,038 kilometres in size, 4.4% larger than California. AlphaWorld is (still) a world of mixed virtual geography, ranging from complex landforms and physical features to sprawling urban areas and suburbia. It centres on Ground Zero, which to all intents and

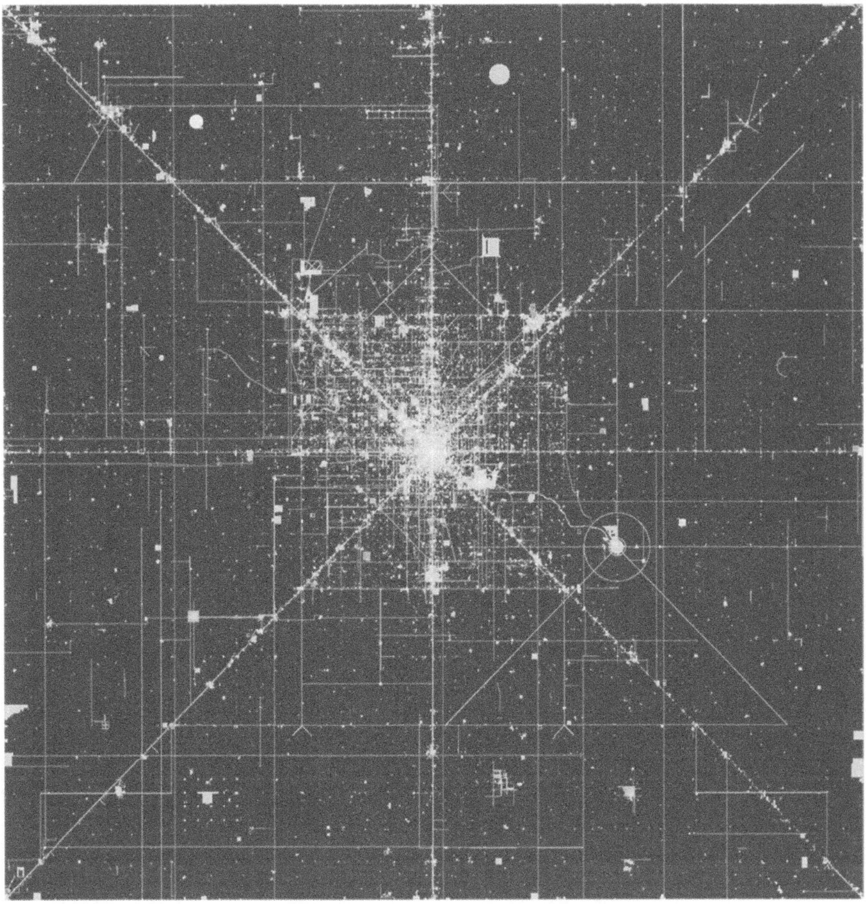

FIGURE 2.5
AlphaWorld density map. *Source*: Credit ActiveWorlds.com.

purposes acts as a Central Business District. Growth away from the centre is on distinct axes focused on the eight compass quadrants as illustrated by the density map in Figure 2.5.

The density map growth along distinct paths is a result of a number of factors, ranging from aspects of agglomeration, natural clustering, and building restrictions. You can see the "starfish" shape of the building as people crowd their buildings along a north-south axis and "equator" of AlphaWorld, and as they build along the coordinates with matching numbers (i.e., 220 N 220 W, 450 S 450 E, etc.). Some do this so that their coordinates are easy to remember, and others simply by building onto what others have built. As in Figure 2.6, these shapes are only visible to those who have access to the Active Worlds servers as they are mapped from data in a similar way to "30 Days in Active Worlds." However, rather than just being the size of Soho

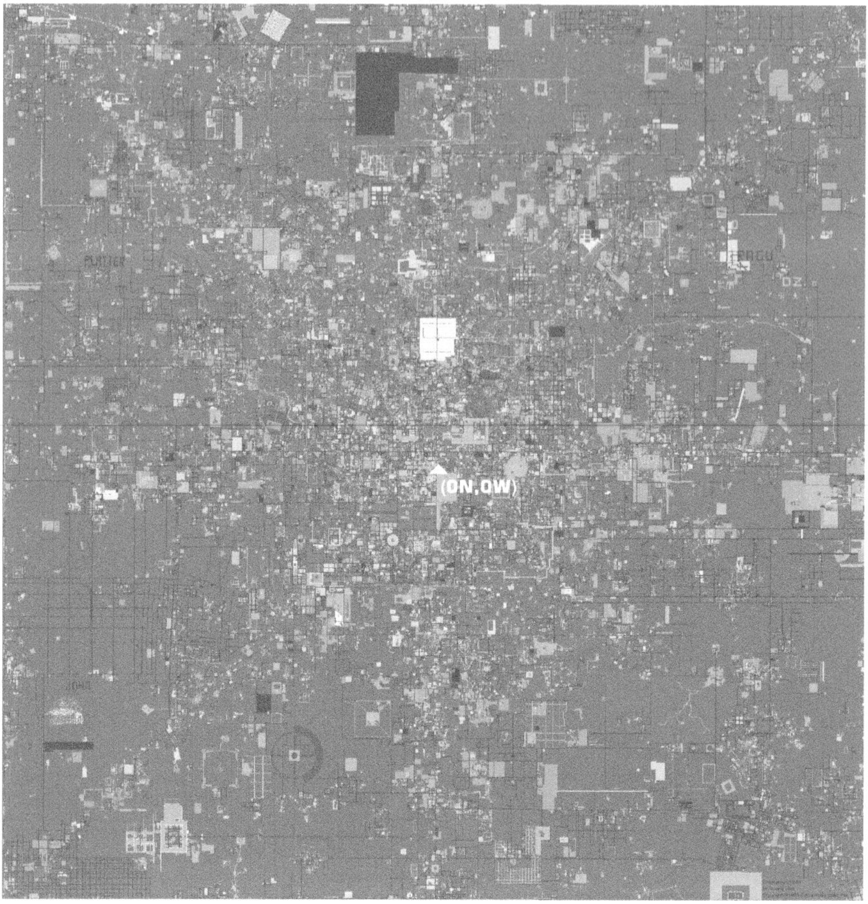

FIGURE 2.6
"Satellite" image of AlphaWorld. Credit ActiveWorlds.com.

in London, as was our case, it covers 429 billion square meters of land- a little larger than California.

The growth of AlphaWorld was remarkable, with 58.5 million objects (Vevo, 1998) placed by over 300,000 citizens. At this point there are about 300,000,000 objects built, the concept and size of Alphaworld truly is breathtaking. A lot of this growth occurred in the heyday of Active Worlds, which was arguably pre-October 1997, before a two-tier structure of citizenship was introduced. Citizens were divided into "tourists" and fee-paying "citizens," with citizenship costing $19.95 per year. As Schroeder and Hudson-Smith noted in 2000, tourists were allowed access to all public spaces just as fee-paying citizens do, but they did not have the same range of choice of avatars and were only able to build in certain areas. In addition to restrictions on building, tourist buildings were not permanent, meaning that any object or building made by a tourist could be deleted by any other user. The introduction of these changes resulted in a decrease in the number of users in AlphaWorlds, and while it provided a more permanent place to build, it also created abandoned wastelands. The buildings built back in its peak days between 1997 and the early 2000s still exist. Indeed, a thread on the social network site Reddit where someone asked if AlphaWorld was still around as two brothers built a house at 33 N 122 W in 1996 notes, "Yes, I found my house. Everything completely the same. 33N 122W," with the reply, "That is overwhelmingly awesome. Twenty-seven years later, the build that you and your brother made is still there. I love to see long-lived video game projects like this sort of thing. Absolutely brilliant; thank you for sharing." As such, we had to log back in ourselves and take a look—the house is indeed still there, although they did not seem to complete the roof (Figure 2.7).

AlphaWorld was arguably the first Metaverse to incorporate sections based on real-world locations. The physical realm is replicated throughout the Metaverse on various scales and levels of realism, ranging from tabletop city views to full-scale replicas. A common example drawn from the real world is the table-sized city model, often utilised by city planners, developers, or for tourism purposes. These models vary in scale from room-sized, allowing for group discussions, to smaller handheld versions.

The capacity to modify scale within the digital environment known as the Metaverse establishes it as an ideal platform for models approximating the proportions of a tabletop. This capability has been explored by our

FIGURE 2.7
Image of a house in AlphaWorld—27 years later at 33 N 122 W. Credit ActiveWorlds.com.

FIGURE 2.8
Tabletop cities in the Metaverse using Adobe Atmosphere. Credit Authors.

laboratory using various Metaverse systems, but most notably using Adobe's short-lived Metaverse initiative, Adobe Atmosphere, spearheaded by the creator of Photoshop and Creative Cloud. We integrated a segment of Central London into the Adobe system and situated it within a larger gallery space. In conjunction with various animations triggered by avatars, the installation enabled users logged in from locations worldwide to insert new building models into the digital representation of London (Figure 2.8).

Adobe Atmosphere launched in 2001 and was sadly discontinued in 2004. Adobe was arguably ahead of its time. It was an innovative system with the ability to import and interact with models.

From London to Tokyo, Dubai, New York, Paris, and Munich, there are representations of nearly every major city in the world within the Metaverse. Venice is one city that has been particularly well-represented, with a number of examples dating back to Active Worlds, onwards to Second Life, VR Chat and more recently Minecraft via Build the Earth which we explore further later. The example in VR Chat is illustrated below, a generally typical example with the bridges, water and landmarks recreated in the digital space (Figure 2.9).

Staying in Venice, there is a trend to link cities and locations in the Metaverse to festivals or events, the La Biennale di Venezia being one of the leaders in the field. Over a century old, La Biennale di Venezia has secured its place as one of the world's most esteemed cultural institutions. Established in 1895, the Biennale now attracts over 500,000 visitors to its Art Exhibition. In the 1930s, new festivals emerged, encompassing Music, Cinema, and Theatre

FIGURE 2.9
Venice in VRChat for the La Biennale. Credit, VRChat.com.

(with the Venice Film Festival in 1932 becoming the inaugural film festival in history). The first International Architecture Exhibition was integrated in 1980, and in 1999, Dance made its debut at La Biennale. In recent years, the institution has ventured into the Metaverse. In 2022, the VRChat system served as the platform for a series of screenings, exhibitions, and events featuring 43 projects from 39 countries, including VR films, VR games, and other immersive experiences, all anchored around a digitally recreated central Venice.

La Biennale consistently demonstrates its commitment to innovation. In 2023, the institution continued to explore the theme of Metaverse experiences. Notably, one specific experience focused on cities and was created by a team of architects with extensive knowledge of urban dynamics and a track record of designing iconic buildings in the physical world. This team included Zaha Hadid Architects and the Chicago-based architecture think tank ArchAgenda. Titled METROTOPIA, the experience aims to establish a unique Metaverse venture dedicated to serving as a virtual communication hub for the global design community (Figures 2.10 and 2.11).

METROTOPIA aspires to become a virtual city, bringing together the function and architecture of a city to fuse design disciplines, including urban design, architecture, interiors, furniture design, product design, fashion design, graphic design, plus related schools, galleries, museums, and exhibitions. With the city's first incubator building and an initial urban core specifically designed by Zaha Hadid, it marks perhaps an early trend of leading architects moving into these emerging new worlds.

While the examples of Venice and London illustrate the mix of user-created content and use of the city for officially sponsored events, more official city-based examples in the Metaverse are emerging; perhaps the most notable is Metaverse Seoul in South Korea. In 2022, South Korea's Ministry

FIGURE 2.10
METROTOPIA by Zaha Hadid Architects and ArchAgenda. Credit Zaha Hadid Architects.

of Science and Information & Communications Technology announced plans to set up a 223.7 billion Korean won (US$180 million) fund to invest in the country's Metaverse industries. The three-part project has a completion date of 2026, with early examples now available to explore. The focus is to create economic, social, and cultural value while also providing access to

FIGURE 2.11
Avatars in METROTOPIA. Credit Zaha Hadid Architects.

government services and public administration. The then President of South Korea, Yoon Suk-yeol, has stated that developing Metaverse-related technology is a national priority. Seoul in South Korea is one of many cities with a developing Metaverse strategy—in a similar way that a city would have a strategy for housing or transport.

One illustrative example of a published strategy is found in the city of Dubai. Titled "The Dubai Metaverse Strategy," the document serves to promote innovation, enhance the economic contributions of the Metaverse through collaborative research and development efforts, and foster advanced ecosystems with the utilisation of accelerators and incubators. Furthermore, it aims to nurture talent and invest in future capabilities by offering comprehensive support in Metaverse education, targeting developers, content creators, and users of digital platforms within the Metaverse community. The strategy also has the objective of developing global standards in the creation of secure platforms for users and establishing Metaverse infrastructure and regulations to facilitate the accelerated adoption of these technologies. Its key pillars encompass extended reality (which merges the physical and virtual realms), AR, VR, mixed reality, and digital twins. Woven together with these are its aspirations to leverage technology to advance technology, creating novel governmental work models and fostering development in critical sectors, including tourism, education, retail, remote work, healthcare, and the legal domain.

The Dubai Metaverse Strategy possesses the goal of transforming Dubai into one of the world's top ten Metaverse economies and a global hub for the Metaverse community. Building upon Dubai's success in attracting over 1,000 companies operating in the fields of blockchain and Metaverse, we explore blockchain in more detail over in the next chapter. It also expresses Dubai's ambitions to support more than 40,000 virtual jobs by 2030. Plans by Dubai and South Korea are focused on not only service provision but also job creation. They are expanding their physical space into the Metaverse to make room for firms to expand and for people to occupy the spaces. It is a bold strategy.

Cities in Games

In a sidestep, gaming in the Metaverse creates standalone worlds often with millions of users. We discuss this more in Chapter 4: Playing the Worlds, but it's worth focusing on one specific example—Minecraft—in terms of creating cities. Minecraft is, as Overby & Jones (2015) note, an open-ended "sandbox" game designed by Markus Persson and published by Mojang where players build constructions of textured cubes in a world with its own laws of physics. It is perhaps the best example of user-created spaces in a gaming environment. Currently owned by Microsoft and available across multiple gaming platforms, according to Microsoft in 2021 there were up to 139 million monthly active players with 238 million copies of the game sold worldwide, with the system only gaining in popularity. These are large numbers of users, and with the world being a predominantly "building" platform, it is expanding faster than any real-world city on Earth. Minecraft can be seen as a series of digital building blocks, LEGO-like to compare it to a real-world toy but operating in boundless space. Milakovic (2021) noted that the dimensions of Minecraft consisted of over 3.6 billion square kilometres or seven times the size of planet Earth. These numbers are worth taking a second look at, as this is only one Metaverse system already more than seven times the dimensions of Planet Earth.

Minecraft falls within the definition of geo-games—games with a spatial aspect. These games are on the boundary of digital twins but with constantly shifting levels of the amount they mirror the real world, like a shimmer of a real-world location coming into and out of focus according to its level of abstraction. Underlining this is the BuildTheEarth (https://buildtheearth.net/) project, where over 210,000 people have participated in one Minecraft mega-project, building a replica of the earth complete with cities block by block. Figure 2.12 illustrates a section of New York under construction. The level of detail is notable, and the time spent building it by users logged in from around the world is laudable.

BuildTheEarth states that their aim is to create a complete 1:1 scale replicate of every building on Earth using Minecraft, a virtual copy of our whole world that showcases the diversity of culture and living space on our planet and stands as a testament for what we can achieve when we work together as a global humanity. They invite every interested player to build with them, to learn from each other about different cultures and about the beauty of the

FIGURE 2.12
New York City in Minecraft as part of BuildTheEarth. Credit BuildTheEarth.

FIGURE 2.13
The Rialto Bridge part of BuildTheEarth. Credit BuildTheEarth.

Earth. They want to make the Earth and its wonders available for anyone with a Minecraft account and invite all explorers and everyone that wants to experience the Earth from the comfort of their home. While building the Earth, they aim to create a global, international community where friendships and collaboration can develop across borders and we can achieve something together as unified humanity. It is a great aim and one that is achieving results, returning to Venice pictured in Figure 2.13 is the Rialto Bridge, again built by many users, collaborating, brick by digital brick to recreate the landmark. In a similar vein, London is also being reconstructed with not only the landmarks but large parts of the city in place. Figure 2.14 highlights Buckingham Palace.

If you want to help build the Earth in Minecraft, then BuildTheEarth notes that the best way you can help is to become a Builder for the project. If you have a copy of Minecraft you are welcome to join in and build a house anywhere in the world. Many people start by building their own neighbourhood or even just their own house and then they go on to build more. They flag not to be scared that you are not good enough to build as we all start with something small. Remember that most houses on Earth are very simple to build and they are there to help you learn how to build more complicated things. It is a brilliant project and one going forward to truly create digital cities in the Metaverse.

As such Minecraft is arguably the most used game for aspects of actual city planning, which could be surprising given its "blocky" nature. Its ease of use and ability to quickly change urban form make cities buildable and adaptable,

FIGURE 2.14
Buckingham Palace part of BuildTheEarth. Credit BuildTheEarth.

yet compared to other games, it is perhaps "less liveable." Minecraft is about building, not so much occupying the worlds; it is like a series of termites building cities and then moving on to the next build.

The Metaverse in the City

The fundamental concept of reality can be substantially altered with the implementation of AR, wherein virtual scenes are superimposed upon the existing physical environment. Presently, AR stands as a distinct concept from the Metaverse; nevertheless, the boundaries between these two realms are gradually diminishing. This is especially true with Metas' recent move into AR glasses in the form of its project "Orion." Project Orion are glasses, that look like everyday glasses but feature a 70-degree projected image into actual space, and while these are still at the point of being a concept device they are expected to enter the market in sometime in 2027 and with it perhaps kickstart the next revolution in mobile spatial computing. As such, it is anticipated that in the near future, the urban landscape as experienced in AR will closely mirror its counterpart within the Metaverse. These converging realities can be characterised as reflective worlds as they not only reflect the physical world but also facilitate the exchange of data and experiences between the two realms.

The genesis of this convergence can arguably be traced back to the advent of the satellite navigation system in automobiles, which facilitated the integration of city maps onto mobile devices. As early as 1981, Honda introduced the Electro Gyrocator, which is widely recognised as the world's first commercially available car navigation system. Subsequent advancements in satellite imagery technologies coupled with ground-based systems for 3D environmental capture have significantly contributed to this convergence. The amalgamation of these technologies has resulted in the development of systems such as Google Earth and Google Street View, which now empower users to access three-dimensional models of cities on their mobile devices.

These models, along with Global Positioning Systems, allow phones to geolocate themselves accurately and ascertain the precise spatial positioning of city buildings and streets in three-dimensional space. In essence, this capability allows for the overlaying of data and graphics onto a video stream captured by the phone's camera, thereby enabling the manipulation of these digital assets in genuine three-dimensional space both in front of and behind buildings. This AR perspective not only facilitates the display of digital content within the urban landscape but also imparts a sense of permanence, as it allows multiple users observing the same space to perceive the identical model. A recent example of this phenomenon is Google's Space Invaders application.

Space Invaders takes the classic game launched in 1978 by TAITO Corporation and uses Google's ARCore Geospatial API, which instantly designs an engaging model onscreen that blends AR and 3D from the nearby environment, including buildings, bridges, and other architectural elements around the player. It also adapts to the layer's real-world location, time, and local weather for immersive gameplay. Space Invaders follows perhaps the most famous AR system—Pokémon Go—which at its peak had over 27 million players, and perhaps more city-focused Minecraft Earth. Minecraft Earth brought the ability to build and create into real-world locations with the ability to collaborate with others. Sadly, it was closed down two years after release due to the then-COVID-19 pandemic limiting people's ability to go out into the real world.

In the realm of the Metaverse, cities are being constructed in a piecemeal manner, comprised of multiple software components. These cities are visualised in diverse ways and frequently duplicated concurrently by numerous individuals. Every city globally possesses numerous 3D models developed by various entities such as municipalities, multinational corporations, architects, local businesses, academics, and interested individuals. In conjunction with these manifold representations, multiple emerging platforms and prominent global companies are now actively engaged in the ongoing transition into the Metaverse. Digital twins are being meticulously crafted, pushing the boundaries of technical capabilities. As Meta aptly observed upon changing its name from Facebook, the Metaverse's full realisation will require a substantial timeframe, likely spanning 10–15 years.

However, we contend that the Metaverse is already taking shape, constructed incrementally by millions of individuals worldwide. From platforms like Active Worlds to a plethora of other systems and games such as Minecraft, the Metaverse is being developed collectively, with settlements and cities gradually emerging within its virtual landscape. The construction of these virtual environments has been a time-consuming endeavour, manually crafted by digital avatars who meticulously shape the digital realms. It is possible that future generations will regard this era as a time of manual labour within the Metaverse, preceding the advent of artificial intelligence and the emergence of automated world-building capabilities. These automated worlds will possess dreamlike qualities while maintaining connections to the real-world cities of today. We will delve further into this topic in Chapter 6. However, before doing so, it is timely that we explore the economic and security considerations pertaining to digital spaces.

References

Milakovic, H. (2021). How big is Minecraft? Is it really bigger than earth. Fiction Horizon. https://fictionhorizon.com/how-big-is-minecraft

Overby, A. & Jones, B. L. (2015). Virtual LEGOs: Incorporating Minecraft into the art education curriculum. Art Education, 68(1), 21–27. https://doi.org/10.1080/00043125.2015.11519302

Radoff, J. (2021). Building the metaverse. Medium. https://medium.com/building-the-metaverse

Vevo (1998). About the AlphaWorld Map. Greg Roelofs and Pieter van der Meulan, Advanced Technology Group at the Philips Multimedia Centre, Palo Alto, California. http://awmap.vevo.com/about.html

3

The Economics and Security of Digital Space

The Metaverse's rapid growth has led to a complex interplay between economics and security. The virtual worlds that comprise the Metaverse are not mere fantasy realms; they are intricately woven into the fabric of our physical reality, giving rise to unique financial ecosystems governed by digital currencies, virtual property ownership, and an entire economy predicated on the trade of non-fungible tokens (NFTs) and digital assets.

This chapter highlights the economic dynamics that underpin the Metaverse, exploring the rise of cryptocurrencies, the emergence of platforms like Decentraland and their native digital economies, and the burgeoning creator economies exemplified by the likes of Fortnite. We also examine the integration of traditional institutions such as the auction house Sotheby's into this new virtual frontier as they recognise the immense potential and real-world value of digital art and collectables.

However, the flourishing economic landscape of the Metaverse also attracts actors and cybercriminals who seek to exploit vulnerabilities for personal gain or ideological agendas. We chronicle one of the earliest documented acts of virtual terrorism, the "Active Worlds Terror Group" attack that threatened to disrupt an entire virtual world, foreshadowing the potential consequences of such attacks in today's economically intertwined Metaverse. Navigating this uncharted digital realm involves grappling with questions of security, privacy, and jurisdiction. How do we safeguard the Metaverse's economic interests while upholding individual freedoms? What legal frameworks are necessary to govern this virtual expanse that transcends national borders, and how can we foster a secure and resilient Metaverse that protects its citizens, assets, and the very fabric of its digital existence?

This chapter explores the captivating, complex, and, at times, contentious intersection of economics and security in the Metaverse, offering insights into the challenges and opportunities that await as we collectively shape the new economics of this digital frontier.

The Economic Landscape of the Metaverse

Underpinning the Metaverse is an intricate web of economic dynamics. It is crucial to acknowledge that nothing is free, as behind the scenes, there

DOI: 10.1201/9781003440437-3

are service companies with servers that require maintenance, staff dedicated to coding the virtual worlds, and bandwidth bills. Consequently, to ensure sustainability, all Metaverse systems require an economic structure. These structures encompass a broad spectrum, ranging from simple advertising models to paid user accounts and even the ability to purchase digital assets and virtual land. As users engage in the digital economy, they facilitate the generation and consumption of virtual goods, services, and experiences. The economic ecosystem within the Metaverse, although in its nascent stage, exhibits increasing parallels to real-world economic systems, encompassing digital real estate, digital art, in-game items, and virtual currency. In essence, it can be viewed as another form of a digital twin, but with a focus on economic aspects. As the adoption of Metaverse systems and technologies gains momentum, new business models will emerge, creating significant economic opportunities. According to Meta, the Metaverse has the potential to contribute substantially to the global economy, with an estimated contribution ranging from US$402 billion to US$760 billion per annum by 2035. This potential is primarily predicted using on the US centred economy, with global growth notably higher, and serves as a compelling reason for the ongoing investments made by companies in Metaverse systems. As such, the economics of the Metaverse is becoming increasingly important.

The virtual economy of the Metaverse is not confined to a single platform; instead, it extends across interconnected virtual worlds, each with its unique rules, currencies, and marketplaces. In many ways, it is like travelling in the real world and moving between countries. This intricate economic landscape has created new challenges and opportunities for businesses, regulators, and consumers alike, as they grapple with novel concepts such as digital asset ownership, scarcity, inflation, and value preservation. As ever with the Metaverse, it is also not new. Second Life was arguably the first true multi-user system to have its own economic structure via the "Linden Dollar." The Linden Dollar is used to purchase digital goods and land, creating with it its own real estate economy in Second Life.

Essentially, the economic system of Second Life is established upon three fundamental principles: a foundational income, the buying and selling of commodities, and the trading of land. Residents of Second Life who are paid members receive a weekly stipend (a basic income) in Linden Dollars, which establishes the baseline economy of the platform. Additional Linden Dollars can be earned through the selling of goods. The ability to engage in buying and selling goods establishes the basis of a contained economic system within Second Life. Initially, Linden Dollars possessed no direct monetary value and were not redeemable for real-world currency by the platform's operator, Linden Lab. If users desired more money for use within the system, they had the option to purchase Linden Dollars directly through a currency exchange. Exchange rates fluctuated, but generally, the value was set at 1 US Dollar to 255 Linden Dollars. This arrangement facilitated the influx of money into the system and by 2009 (arguably the height of Second Life's popularity) the economy had amassed a value of $567 million. This phenomenon necessitates further analysis—individuals were exchanging real-world money for a virtual currency within the Metaverse to purchase plots of land, construct dwellings, and acquire assets for their avatars.

As a lab, we moved into Second Life in 2006, setting up a space kindly provided to us by the Nature Publishing Group. Nature had "Nature Island," allowing various research groups around the world to explore Second Life and its implications for a whole number of applications, which ranged from simulated biology and through to our work on cities and urban structure in the Metaverse (Figure 3.1).

The financial outlay associated with acquiring an island within Second Life fluctuates, with an average initial investment of approximately US$350 for the land itself, followed by an ongoing monthly obligation of $295, which may be interpreted as a form of property tax. Numerous individuals opt to purchase islands and subsequently lease the land, thereby establishing a secondary economy within Second Life predicated upon the landlord-renter dynamic. It could be argued that acquiring land in Second Life is akin to renting, as the purchaser is essentially securing space on a server that may potentially be discontinued, resulting in the forfeiture of their virtual property. As we were kindly provided by Nature, the only assets we were required to procure were those pertaining to our avatars. Analogous to the majority of Metaverse systems, avatars in Second Life possess the capability to be customised with new garments, eyewear, headwear, footwear, and so forth as detailed in Chapter 2. These digital designs are uploaded into the system

FIGURE 3.1
CASA in Second Life on Nature Island. Credit Authors.

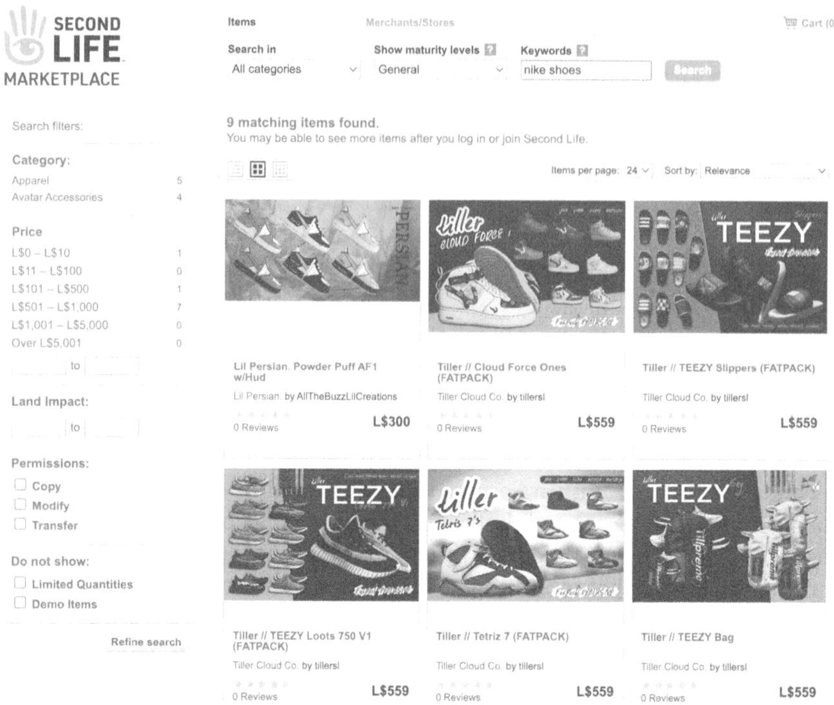

FIGURE 3.2
Merchandise and clothing in Second Life. Credit Second Life.

and subsequently offered for sale by merchants within Second Life. They serve as the virtual equivalents of clothing stores and, akin to the real world, certain "brands" are present. However, during the early stages, established brands were slow to recognise the potential inherent in this virtual realm, thus creating an opportunity for a robust exchange in digital replications of well-known brands. A wide array of items ranging from Nike trainers to Prada glasses were available to buy, none of them officially sanctioned, yet existing in an economy worth hundreds of thousands of dollars (Figure 3.2).

My avatar in Second Life had a zebra-like jacket, a blonde spiky haircut, and black-rimmed glasses, all paid for via converting British Pounds into Linden Dollars. The haircut cost the equivalent of £15, which at that time was more than I was paying for a real-world haircut. As noted before, there is a valuable life lesson there, although maybe not in economics.

The virtual economy of Second Life acts as an instance for examining the economic principles that govern the Metaverse. The development of Linden Dollars, a self-contained virtual currency, and a dependable currency exchange system enabled Second Life inhabitants to actively contribute to a dynamic and self-governing economic ecosystem. The substantial monetary activities taking place in this virtual setting serve as a testament to the potential and significance of the Metaverse in reshaping how commerce and virtual interactions unfold in the future. Notably, the advent of cryptocurrencies marked a pivotal juncture, establishing a direct connection between the economics of the Metaverse and the real-world economy.

The Crypto Economy

Cryptocurrency as a concept is trying to revolutionise the realm of finance, signifying a paradigm shift in our comprehension of currency and transactional processes. This transformation has extended beyond the physical world into the Metaverse, where the impact of cryptocurrencies has been profound. These digital or virtual currencies leverage cryptographic techniques—methods and mathematical algorithms employed for data security during communications and transactions—to facilitate secure financial exchanges, ensuring enhanced privacy, transparency, and decentralisation. In contrast to traditional currencies controlled by governments—known as fiat currencies—cryptocurrencies operate independently of any central authority, with transactions recorded on a distributed ledger known as the blockchain. It is this non-governmental autonomous nature of cryptocurrency that has enabled the Metaverse to transition from systems such as the Linden Dollar, essentially a fiat currency, to a global financial system.

The inception of this revolution can be traced back to 2009 when Bitcoin, arguably the inaugural and most celebrated cryptocurrency, was introduced by Satoshi Nakamoto (presumed to be a pseudonymous person or persons). Bitcoin pioneered the concept of peer-to-peer electronic cash systems, functioning as a decentralised digital currency that facilitates direct transactions, transcending not only governmental authorities but also banking institutions. Each Bitcoin transaction is permanently recorded on the blockchain—an immutable and transparent ledger (a record-keeping system) maintained by a network of computers known as nodes. The process of validating transactions, termed mining, entails solving complex mathematical puzzles. Miners, utilising their own computers, are rewarded with newly minted bitcoins for their efforts. Bitcoin's finite supply, capped at 21 million coins, creates a deflationary nature, contributing to its allure as a store of value. While the concept may initially appear intricate, it essentially involves the exchange and validation of currency, enabling individuals to engage in the acquisition and disposal of goods. Furthermore, cryptocurrencies can be bought and sold in exchange for traditional currencies such as the dollar, pound, and euro. The current global market value of cryptocurrency exceeds 3 trillion US Dollars, albeit it remains a volatile market subject to increasing regulatory scrutiny from governments.

Bitcoin's success has spurred the creation of numerous alternative cryptocurrencies, collectively referred to as altcoins. Each altcoin is designed with distinct features and applications, catering to diverse industries and addressing specific issues. While the Linden Dollar remains confined to the virtual realm of Second Life, it has now established a connection with Bitcoin, thereby bridging the economic chasm between the closed system and the external world.

Non-Fungible Tokens (NFTs)

The landscape of the digital economy is fast moving, creating opportunities for new innovations but also risks for those who invest. Non-Fungible Tokens, known as NFTs, are the current economic innovation impacting the Metaverse as they are made to enable the exchange of digital assets, allowing a sense of ownership of digital artworks, 3D objects (think my £15 haircut in Second Life), and allowing the authentication of the provenance of digital creations. Unlike what crazily could be called "traditional cryptocurrencies" that are interchangeable and hold equal value, NFTs represent one-of-a-kind assets, each possessing distinct characteristics and attributes. The shift in the use of currencies in the Metaverse moves us away from Second Life and into systems set up directly to make use of emerging cryptocurrencies and NFTs, most significantly in Decentraland.

Decentraland

Decentraland is a decentralised virtual world built on blockchain technology where NFTs play a fundamental role in defining ownership of assets in the world and creating the basis of its economic ecosystem. The platform's native currency, known as MANA, an altcoin, is used to purchase virtual land and other digital assets, with NFTs allowing users to own and trade unique parcels of virtual land, art, wearables, and other digital items. Each parcel of virtual land is represented by an NFT, providing verifiable proof of ownership recorded on the blockchain. Users can purchase these virtual parcels in Decentraland's virtual marketplace using MANA. Once acquired, landowners have the freedom to develop their virtual properties, hosting events, building structures, and monetising their creations. It can all seem a little complicated, but to break it down, it's like buying a house in the real world: you would purchase the house with money (just swap Pounds/Dollars/Euros with MANA) and you receive the Deeds to the House, a document proving ownership, whereas in Decentraland this is an NFT.

In essence, the Decentraland economy operates in a decentralised (thus the name) and transparent manner, wholly governed by smart contracts and NFT ownership. As users engage in transactions, buying, selling, and developing virtual properties, all activities are recorded on the blockchain, creating a publicly accessible ledger of the virtual economy's activities, allowing the ability to buy or rent land to operate. As such, and returning to the house

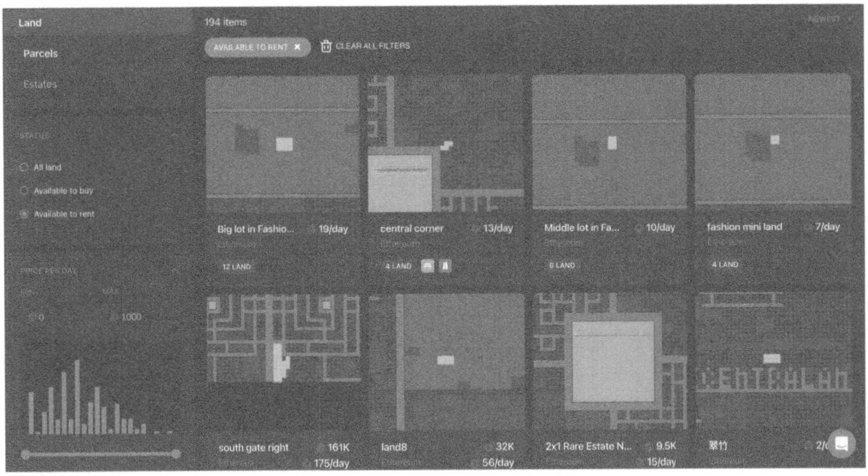

FIGURE 3.3
Land available in Decentraland. Credit Decentraland.

concept but in this case land to build a house, there is an active economy in buying or renting land. Figure 3.3 illustrates the newest land in Decentraland available to rent with its cost per day. As in the real world, land prices vary by location, shape, and size.

The Central Corner plot pictured in Figure 3.4 is available to rent for the equivalent of $5 a day or $1800 a year. These prices fluctuate according to the value of the exchange market.

FIGURE 3.4
A plot of land for $1800 a year. Credit Decentraland.

FIGURE 3.5
Decentraland. Credit Decentraland.

Decentraland is compartmentalised into 90,601 distinct parcels known as LAND, each of which is symbolised by a NFT. Each parcel encompasses an area of 16 square metres (virtually) and possesses a unique location with coordinates within the system. Consequently, it bears similarity to other systems such as Active Worlds and Second Life, which utilise land parcels and a coordinate system for their placement. The aggregate economic value of Decentraland fluctuates in accordance with the prevailing exchange rate of MANA. Analogous to Bitcoin, there is a finite quantity of MANA available (2.2 billion) with 1.8 billion currently in circulation. At the time of writing, MANA's market capitalisation stands at $700 million, approximately equivalent to the gross domestic product of Tonga.

The NFTs representing digital art, land, and wearables within Decentraland introduce a transformative paradigm for artists, creators, and users seeking to engage in land transactions. Artists possess the ability to tokenise their digital assets as NFTs, thereby providing collectors with verifiable proof of ownership and establishing a means to trade their unique creations. In certain respects, this can be likened to an arts and crafts marketplace reminiscent of its real-world counterpart, Etsy (Figure 3.5).

Oncyber.io

While we are exploring economic systems in the Metaverse, it is worth looking at one of the more recent emerging systems known as Oncyber. Timelines in the Metaverse are increasingly listed in months as more systems develop. Oncyber is a browser-based Metaverse system with small-scale standalone environments together via portals. The scale is from a local urban square through to a gallery space or room. The whole system is heavily gallery and music-focused, with the ability to show and sell NFT artworks. We thought it was worth mentioning as it is rather good and well worth a look by heading to https://oncyber.io/

The company was founded in 2022 with seed funding of $6,700,000 from a small number of investors. It was specifically developed around the ability to let artists and collectors construct and sell their 3D virtual showrooms for NFTs. Alongside this, it has developed a subculture around music with events held where avatars will gather to dance and hang out with like-minded people. The avatars as such are not your typical Metaverse avatar, they are specifically optimised to allow mass gathering in small spaces. The avatars have graphically simplistic shared synced motions, allowing large groups of people to be displayed, with one event in April 2023 attracting 3,500 avatars from 100 countries squeezed into a space to dance.

At the moment, it is free to join and build in Oncyber.io and a number of high-quality spaces are available to buy, again via a cryptocurrency system. This is a notable difference: the spaces available to buy are not land, but ready to go architecturally designed locations. So rather than spending funds on haircuts and clothes, you can spend on the best-quality spaces and places to show art, play music, or show your portfolio of work.

One of the founders of Oncyber in a series of tweets (as they were still called then) noted that their dream Metaverse is 5,000 self-governing districts in 10 self-governing cities in one self-governing world. Linking back to our previous chapter on cities in the Metaverse, this perhaps truly points to the future: a series of self-governing cities that in themselves have 500 districts all linked to a cryptocurrency.

The focus of Oncyber has been on an artistic future. Art features heavily in the economics of the Metaverse, so much so that one of the world's oldest and most respected auction houses (Sotheby's) is now trading in the Metaverse.

Sotheby's Metaverse

In Sotheby's own words, they were established in 1744 and are the world's largest, most trusted, and dynamic marketplace for art and luxury. They empower an international community of collectors and connoisseurs to discover, acquire, finance, and consign fine art and rare objects. Their reputation for trust and authenticity is backed by a global network of specialists spanning 40 countries and 44 departments which include Contemporary Art, Modern and Impressionist Art, Old Masters, Chinese Works of Art, jewellery, watches, wine and spirits, and interiors, among many others. As such an established and traditional institution, it is therefore refreshing that you can also find them in Decentraland. Yet unlike the showcase location in Central London, where you can be met by a doorman, in Decentraland there is a

FIGURE 3.6
Sotheby's Opens in Decentraland. Credit Sotherby's.

yellow digital avatar of an ape who will greet you at the door. The space was launched in early 2020 as a "twin" of the London establishment, rebuilt and reimagined in Decentraland (Figure 3.6).

In 2021, the contemporary art market witnessed a significant transformation due to the emergence of NFTs, which rapidly gained prominence. Sotheby's, through a series of innovative initiatives and auctions, played a pivotal role in this wave. Notably, the launch of Sotheby's Metaverse, a digitally native trading platform designed to be user-friendly, marked a significant milestone. The decision to engage in long-term investments in the cryptoart space resulted from an initial partnership with the marketplace platform Nifty Gateway. Max Moore, who serves as the head of contemporary art auctions at Sotheby's Asia, highlighted the remarkable success of the first NFT sale in April, featuring the artist Pak and generating a total of $17 million. This sale exemplified the substantial demand from collectors and the high quality of artwork from artists, underscoring the immense potential of this burgeoning market. Recognising Sotheby's current position in the contemporary art market and its expertise in bridging the gap between the physical and digital realms, Moore emphasised the crucial role Sotheby's could play in this evolving landscape. Building on this discussion, Molly Nelson, assistant vice-president of Sotheby's Advisory, acknowledged the entry into Decentraland as a bold step into the previously uncharted territory of digital art while also representing a natural extension of Sotheby's longstanding commitment to various art forms. Nelson expressed enthusiasm for the exploration of not only the fine art of NFTs but also diverse verticals such as music, entertainment, and sports. Sotheby's Metaverse aims to provide a comprehensive platform that enables collectors to explore a wide range of options, thus consolidating Sotheby's position as a one-stop destination for art enthusiasts.

Sotheby's is a clear example of recognising the shift in the economics of digital collectables and using its heritage and trust of users to make a mark in the Metaverse, innovating and building on the establishment from 1744 to create a new boundary between real and digital in terms of digital collections. It should be noted that the economics of the Metaverse, especially when linked to NFTs, is volatile. At the time of editing this section (April 2025), the market cap of NFTs is worth $60.4 billion, yet it does not really register in the mainstream world. It exists on the frontier, shaping the way we interact, trade, and experience digital assets within the virtual landscape.

Fortnite

Before we move on more broadly into Security and the Metaverse, it is worth examining a system which some would argue is on the edge of the Metaverse and others would argue is the future of the Metaverse—Fortnite. We explore Fortnite more in Chapter 4 "Playing the Worlds: Gaming and the Metaverse," but it is worth highlighting for its economic landscape. Fortnite, developed by Epic Games, has grown from a mere game into a cultural phenomenon with notable economic implications. In essence, it is a cooperative shooter-survival game where the last person standing wins the game, all set in a lush landscape with console-quality graphics. What sets Fortnite apart is its monetisation strategies, the development of an in-game economy, and its evolving relationship with the broader concept of the Metaverse.

At its essence, Fortnite operates on a free-to-play basis. It is accessible across a multitude of platforms, spanning from personal computers to a variety of mobile devices, PlayStation, Xbox, and Nintendo Switch. Players are not required to incur any financial expenditure or make purchases in order to download and engage in the game. This fundamental aspect serves as an enticement into the gaming ecosystem. Within this system, players have the option to partake in the economy by utilising V-Bucks, which function as Fortnite's virtual currency. V-Bucks can be employed to acquire cosmetic items such as character skins, emotes, and other in-game commodities that do not confer any gameplay advantages. The absence of such advantages ensures that the game remains competitive for all participants, irrespective of their financial investments. This approach bears similarities to other previously examined systems, such as Second Life, albeit Fortnite has elevated this concept to unprecedented heights, primarily attributable to the generation of a desire among players rather than a necessity. By consistently introducing novel and exclusive cosmetic items, frequently drawing inspiration from popular culture (e.g., skins of Marvel superheroes or pop star Ariana Grande), players are motivated to purchase V-Bucks. Additionally, Fortnite incorporates a seasonal structure, characterised by evolving themes and narratives. This approach ensures that the content remains fresh and encourages sustained player engagement.

Within the context of Fortnite Creative mode, a thriving creator economy exists. This mode enables players to design and construct their own islands and games within Fortnite. This user-generated content not only enhances the replay value of the game but also establishes Fortnite as a platform rather than just a game. It serves as a virtual space for social interaction, creativity, and commerce. Epic Games' creators, as part of the Creator Economy 2.0 initiative, have the opportunity to generate revenue based on the engagement their islands receive within Fortnite Creative. Engagement is determined by various metrics, such as the number of players visiting an island, the frequency at which an island is played, and the duration players spend on an island. As part of this arrangement, creators receive a share of 40% of Epic Games' net revenue from Fortnite each month. Thus, players create content for Epic through its platform, utilising various tools ranging from a system within Fortnite to a more complex external game engine import pathway (known as Unreal). Fortnite's revenue stream is estimated to be around $2.5 billion, with 40% of this amount (minus processing fees) going directly to creators, resulting in an approximate value of $750 million.

Within these virtual worlds, there are substantial economic systems operating with incomes surpassing the gross domestic product of certain real-world countries. It is significant to recognise that virtual worlds generate more economic income than nation-states, despite their substantial populations. Presently, each of these economic systems operates independently, although there is some overlap with the real world in terms of financial transactions, but not between virtual worlds. A cross-Metaverse currency does not currently exist and indeed may never, but as we alluded to, travelling in the real world and using different currencies, the Metaverse is the same, with some worlds now holding notable economic values.

Security

The financial well-being of the Metaverse is intrinsically intertwined with its security measures. The burgeoning virtual economies, coupled with the tangible real-world value accorded to digital assets, amplify the risks associated with any security breaches. Consequently, the establishment of a robust and resilient security infrastructure that safeguards the Metaverse's security, its intricate systems, and the avatars within its virtual space is fundamental to its long-term viability.

Furthermore, the advent of digital spaces introduces a novel dimension of cybersecurity concerns. The blurring of boundaries between virtual and physical realities raises profound ethical and legal questions, as cyberattacks within the Metaverse have the potential to trigger real-world repercussions. Addressing these complex issues necessitates a harmonious interplay between the virtual and real worlds from a legal standpoint. It also requires a comprehensive understanding of the multifaceted nature of security breaches and the potential manifestations of terrorism within the Metaverse.

Terrorism in Active Worlds

One of the earliest documented terrorist attacks on the Metaverse occurred in our own "30 Days in Active Worlds" project. In the initial chapter, we investigated the community and structures that emerged as a result of the long-term experiment. Our server, which hosted the world, was simply a personal desktop computer, a Dell Windows PC located beneath our desk. It housed the locations and spaces that made up the world and welcomed avatars as they entered. As part of a university research laboratory, it was also subject to various security measures to prevent cybersecurity breaches.

Returning to the narrative from Chapter 1 "The Early Frontier," on Day 4, while seated at our desk in the basement of a building owned by University College London, we received 25 email messages and a stream of ICQ messages. ICQ, an online messaging system established in 1996 and later acquired by America Online (AOL) in 1998, was utilised as a telegram messaging system—think of it as an early precursor to Twitter (or X as it's now known). The messages complained about a user in the world who was demolishing structures and placing thousands of objects.

It became apparent that a user was causing havoc, placing numerous objects and appearing intent to overload our server, effectively destroying the world. A few minutes after logging into our email, the server abruptly shut down, causing the world to go offline. The world had vanished from the Active Worlds Universe, and it was only Day 4.

Upon examining the log files, we noticed that a single user had been logging on and off during the night and, over a period of more than five hours, placing over 85,000 objects in the world. The objects had been placed using automatic building software called "hambot," which had been banned in some regions of the AW Universe, but not in ours, as users could say and build whatever they wanted. Bots in Active Worlds were early examples of Automated Assistants, a very basic form of Artificial Intelligence formed by a series of rules programmed into their system. As such, they were able to carry out tasks such as acting as tourist guides to answer questions about the world, greeting users automatically as they teleported into a new location, or building on behalf of users and placing objects. These bots would often have the form of an Avatar; even back in 1998, the first glimpses of automatically constructed worlds were beginning to appear.

As our world was a world without laws (beyond our now 1st law of no pornography), we allowed automated building bots, and if a user wanted to place 85,000 objects, they were allowed to do so. However, because it had crashed the main server and thus essentially ended the 30 Days project, we decided that the objects that had been placed would be cleared up and the community would be put to a vote to see if they wanted additional laws put into place to protect the world. Luckily, the layout of the world was actually defined by a small text file on the server; as such, it was a relatively easy task to search for the objects placed by the bot, remove them, and restore the world to its pre-attack state.

Each morning, a detailed map of the world was created using a traditional top-down perspective in order to track growth. The 85,000 rogue objects were mapped and subsequently published on our news page. Following this, a new text file was uploaded, the world was restored, the server was rebooted, and 30 Days in Active Worlds was brought back online. Within a minute of the world going live, users began to arrive and assess the damage. Structures constructed by tourists had been demolished, and a trail of destruction was evident across the world, reminiscent of the aftermath of an earthquake. A group gathered near Ground Zero and engaged in discussions regarding the nature of the perpetrator responsible for such an act. One of the users posited that the incident may have been intentionally orchestrated during the logging process as a form of publicity stunt to gauge the reactions of the population. Suddenly, as avatars encircled we found ourselves as the prime suspect.

Despite the virtual nature of the environment, we came to the realisation that discomfort was still a palpable emotion. As the avatars congregated around us, accusations were swiftly and relentlessly hurled our way. Through extensive diplomacy, we endeavoured to persuade the users to adopt our perspective, emphasising the futility of such destructive acts within our own creation. However, the seeds of doubt had already been sown. The occurrence of vandalism during Lorca's (the journalist who took up a long term stay with us during the project) presence in the world garnered significant attention from prominent online platforms such as the Press Association, TescoNet, and Excite, which were among the most widely visited user and news websites at the time. While this attention did indeed heighten interest in "30 Days in Active Worlds," it simultaneously exacerbated the mistrust prevalent within the community. Paradoxically, this shift in the level of trust, or perhaps as a direct consequence thereof, led the relatively small but steadily growing community to unanimously endorse a new law, complemented by the establishment of a dedicated police department equipped with call boxes and regular patrols. In essence, by the conclusion of Day 4, a second law prohibiting the presence of bots had been enacted, along with the creation of a modest police force.

Once restarted, the world remained incident-free, with a growing population building, chatting, and generally going about their business. Until that is, on Day 9, when a tourist going under the name of Jero logged into the world. Via the now common regular patrols, Jero attracted the attention of Betty B, who was by then a core member of the community. Jero was asking questions about the vandalism incident from Day 4, and it became evident from the nature of Jero's conversation that he had been involved in the incident. Betty B sent us an ICQ message; upon logging into the world, we were greeted by Jero. He divulged proudly that he was the "High Commander of the Active Worlds Terrorist Group" and, although he had not undertaken the vandalism himself, he had issued orders for it to occur. Jero then issued a series of threats that he would hack into the main server hosting 30 Days in Active Worlds and shut the world down. I sent a message to all the known users in the world that the world was on "Def Con One" (a military alert) status, with a new attack imminent. A group gathered at Ground Zero, looking towards the skyline and waiting to see what would happen.

While Jero was logged on, a trace was carried out on his IP number (his internet address identifier), and the company behind Active Worlds was informed of the threat. This was mainly to ensure that the main world server couldn't be hacked, as this would have jeopardised our local network at University College London. As a result of the IP trace, Active Worlds contacted the Internet Service Provider (ISP) of Jero and obtained a contact number for the user's account. The information was provided by the ISP due to a number of complaints that Active Worlds had had in relation to several recurring IP numbers. Apparently, the Terrorist Group had been quite active in the preceding months. Active Worlds contacted Jero, or to be more precise, Jero's father in Vancouver, Canada.

Legal action was threatened, and Jero, who it turned out was a 15-year-old teenager logged in from his bedroom, had his computer taken away from him. The computer was not removed from Jero, however, before he could issue one final threat. Jero logged into 30 Days in Active Worlds for one last time on Day 11. He teleported to our location and issued the threat that we had upset the wrong person and the group would be taking imminent action against my lab. Knowing he posed no serious threat, I ejected him from the world and thought that that would be the last I saw of him. Within half an hour, we had lost all internet access from my personal machine at University College London. The world remained online, but we couldn't even pick up my email. We remained unable to connect for over six hours while my internet connection was restored—a hacker had entered my machine via my own personal web server and disabled all our network card settings. Jero had, in some way, had the final say.

A final say until we jump forward to 2025. Just before concluding this chapter, I received an email message out of the blue with a darknet address (a special-use top-level domain suffix designating an anonymous hidden service) asking if I remembered the attack, stating—

> *I hope you realise the implications of what happened back in those days. We were the first in the "Metaverse" to overlap the real world. Like our avatars met in a virtual world and I was able to get inside your computer and affect your real life, even take your time away. As everything is connected now with augmented reality and the Metaverse, connected homes, etc. The Metaverse will overlap with the real world soon.*

After a few more emails passed between us, Jero wanted to tell his side of the story.

Jero's Story

Written in his own words—Growing up in a rough neighbourhood filled with poverty and crime, he had created a persona for himself, calling himself "Jero." Jero always felt out of place. Despite the odds stacked against him, however, he refused to let his circumstances define him. Instead, he turned to computers and networking technologies as an escape, spending countless hours tinkering with hardware and software alike. At first, he found himself with a computer found in the trash behind a business he used to ride his bicycle for hours as an escape from his circumstances; an old discarded computer intrigued his mind. Being only 13 years old, he had little means of his own to ever purchase such a marvel of technology. When "Jero" came across an old 386 computer in the garbage bin outside a business, he couldn't help but feel drawn to it. Having grown up in poverty, Jero had few resources available to him beyond what he could find or create on his own. So when he spotted the discarded machine, something inside him stirred.

Curious about the device, Jero brought it home and started tinkering with it. With only a basic understanding of computing, he was surprised to discover that the machine still held some value. In fact, he noticed that it contained a modem capable of connecting to online services via telephone lines. It wasn't until Jero saw some graffiti advertising a phone number that he realised the true potential of this old tech. Following the instructions scrawled on the wall, Jero dialled the provided number and connected to his very first Bulletin Board System (BBS), which was a primitive form of online forum where users communicated through text messages. Jero's initial encounter with the BBS world was exhilarating—he was suddenly transported into a whole new universe filled with games, chats, and forums dedicated to a wide variety of topics. One particular game caught Jero's attention: an old text-based RPG known as "Lord." As Jero delved deeper into the game, he became increasingly enamoured with the possibilities presented by this newfound realm. For the first time in his life, he felt a sense of agency over his own destiny; he could craft his own character, explore virtual landscapes, and interact with others around the globe.

It was through this game that Jero truly fell in love with the transformative power of technology and the boundless horizons opened up by digital connection. Looking back, Jero credits his chance discovery of that ancient computer and his subsequent introduction to BBS culture as pivotal moments in shaping his future path towards becoming an advocate for inclusive digital governance and promoting greater accessibility to technology for all. As Jero continued to immerse himself in the world of computers and technology, he quickly realised that his outdated equipment wouldn't cut it forever. The limitations of his old 386dx33 personal computer and 14.4 kilobits a second modem left much to be desired, especially as he began to learn more about the wonders of the emerging internet. Determined to keep up with the latest developments, Jero turned to a somewhat unconventional solution: pirated software. Using his connections on the BBS systems, he was able to get access to what they called Warez (pirated games); he began downloading copies of popular games, getting a cheap source of floppy disks, and reselling them to other students who lacked the financial means to purchase them legally. This venture proved successful, allowing Jero to earn enough money to invest in a newer, more powerful PC, a 486dx/66 with a 28.8 modem. With his new system, Jero was finally able to connect directly to the internet, opening up a whole new realm of possibility. As he explored the fledgling web, he marvelled at its potential—not just as a platform for communication and information sharing, but also as a tool for social change and community building. Jero recognised that not everyone had equal access to these opportunities, however, particularly those in lower-income communities like his own. Drawing upon his own experiences, he began advocating for greater equity and accessibility in digital spaces, calling for policies that would bridge the so-called "digital divide," becoming a sort of digital activist. Throughout his journey, Jero remained committed to using technology as a force for positive social impact, working tirelessly to promote greater equality and opportunity in a rapidly evolving landscape. His early experiences with pirated software may have been less than orthodox but ultimately served as a catalyst for his larger mission of creating a more equitable and accessible digital world where there was a version of the human rights charter online.

Discovering the Metaverse, it wasn't long before he realised his voice was not being heard through normal activism or trying to communicate his concerns to those he reached out to, emailing multimillionaires trying to create a digital advocacy group. With no success, he was powerful in technology and skill but poor, that is when he stumbled upon a virtual Metaverse called Active Worlds. Despite his growing skill at hacking and skill at influencing others and his passionate commitment to advancing causes related to digital inclusion and social justice, Jero found that his voice often went unheard when he tried to make his case via traditional forms of activism or by reaching out directly to influential figures in the field. Emailing multi-millionaires or influential figures in the tech sphere with no results, frustrated by what seemed like a deafening silence from many of the industry's most prominent players, Jero resolved to find another way to effect real change. Intrigued by the concept of Active Worlds, Jero saw an opportunity to use this new medium to build a community focused on promoting digital democracy, transparency, and innovation. Jero's critique of the citizenship system in Active Worlds stemmed from his belief that it perpetuated inequality and undermined the spirit of openness and freedom that underpinned the game's design philosophy.

As someone who strongly identified with Marxist and communist ideals, Jero viewed the existence of a tiered membership structure—which granted certain privileges and benefits exclusively to paying members—as fundamentally unfair and antithetical to the game's purported ethos. For Jero, the notion that individuals should have to pay to enjoy full access and participation within a virtual community ran contrary to the idea that such spaces ought to be accessible to all, regardless of their financial circumstances. He believed that the presence of a monetary barrier constituted a form of exclusion, denying less fortunate players the same opportunities and experiences afforded to wealthier ones. Moreover, Jero also felt that the existence of a privileged citizen class created divisions and hierarchies within the community, further exacerbating existing inequalities and reinforcing preconceived prejudices. To him, this was antithetical to the idea of creating a fairer, more equitable society and served primarily to reinforce the status quo. Thus, when Jero assumed command of Active Worlds Terrorist Group (AWT), he vowed to challenge this system head-on, arguing that it was no longer tenable given the evolving nature of digital communities and networks. Instead, he proposed a more egalitarian model, one that prioritised inclusivity, transparency, and democratic decision-making above profit and commercial interests.

Ultimately, however, Jero's efforts to reform the system encountered strong resistance from other stakeholders, including long-standing administrators and investors who felt that their economic interests were threatened by his proposals. This led to a protracted conflict between Jero and the established order within Active Worlds, ultimately culminating in his terrorist attack on the world. Created by CASA "30 Days in Active Worlds," he felt with his actions he could force the company that ran the service to change its ways, threatening further attacks inside the virtual Metaverse if they did not comply. This is the story of the first documented Metaverse hacker and terrorist in a virtual world.

After the Attack

The virtual terror attack carried out by Jero's terrorist cell within the confines of Active Worlds made headlines around the world, marking what many considered to be a new frontier in the ever-evolving landscape of modern-day terrorism. The details of the attack, which involved disrupting critical infrastructure and causing widespread chaos and destruction inside the virtual world, were reported widely across mainstream media channels, including Associated Press and Yahoo News. Following the investigation into Jero's activities in Active Worlds, the Royal Canadian Mounted Police (RCMP) and Federal Bureau of Investigation (FBI) took drastic measures against the teenage activist. Not only did they visit his family's residence, but they also threatened charges of industrial sabotage against him for his alleged role in perpetrating a virtual terror attack. This severe consequence underscored the seriousness of the issue and the potential legal ramifications associated with engaging in such conduct. As a result of these developments, Jero lost access to the internet for several years. The authorities seized his computer during the investigation and he never got it back, effectively cutting off his connectivity to the digital world. While some might argue that this measure was disproportionately harsh, given the fact that the attack itself was virtual, it highlights the complex legal framework governing cybersecurity issues and the evolving nature of criminal liability in the age of technology. Moreover, it serves as a chilling warning to other would-be cybercriminals or virtual vigilantes who seek to leverage advanced virtual environments for personal gain or political advantage. Ultimately, the episode raises important questions regarding the limits of freedom of expression and assembly in the context of emerging technologies, particularly those pertaining to privacy, data protection, and intellectual property rights.

It was nice to hear from Jero, although it also made us a little nervous. Our correspondence was short, but it highlighted the feeling and nature of the Metaverse in those early frontier days. Pushing against the system is part of the frontier mentality; Jero just pushed in a different way. The involvement of the FBI and the Royal Canadian Mounted Police was regrettable; however, if the same happened today, the response would be similar, although perhaps on a larger scale given the economies at stake in a terrorist attack in the Metaverse. Nowadays, your IP address can be easily hidden, so it would be much harder (almost impossible) to track a hacker down.

Crimes committed within the Metaverse resemble those encountered in the broader expanse of the internet, encompassing activities such as money laundering, data theft (inclusive of digital assets), digital impersonation, ransomware, sexual harassment, assault, and as has been observed, broader acts of terrorism directed against specific locales and spaces. However, the nature of these crimes within the Metaverse presents additional complexities due to their occurrence within a three-dimensional environment that transcends traditional geographical borders and jurisdictions. At present, The Law Commission of England and Wales is engaged in a comprehensive review entitled "Digital Assets: Which Court of Law?" This review is necessitated by the fact that individuals within the Metaverse can simultaneously exist in multiple locations, including their physical login location, the digital location of the virtual world they inhabit, and the geographical location of the server hosting the virtual world. Consequently, an individual's apparent location in America, as indicated by their login details, may not accurately reflect their actual physical location, which could be in the United Kingdom or any other part of the globe. The use of Virtual Private Networks (VPNs) has become increasingly prevalent, primarily driven by two considerations: the desire to conceal one's geographical location and the need to access services that may be restricted or unavailable in one's own country.

Within the Metaverse, users are typically not required to disclose their geographic location, and such location may not be pertinent to any transactions. Consequently, it is challenging to associate events or assets with a specific legal system or set of laws. For instance, a user selling a virtual land parcel may be situated in Spain, while the buyer is in Canada, and the server hosting the transaction is located in New York. In the event of a dispute that cannot be resolved by the company operating the system, it becomes unclear which court in which country would have jurisdiction over the matter. This situation reflects an evolving landscape where national legal systems are striving to adapt, as exemplified by the ongoing review being conducted in the United Kingdom.

In conjunction with and supplementing national laws, each company's terms and conditions must be agreed to before accessing a particular world. Essentially, you are entering a private space where, just as in the physical world with local ordinances, you must adhere to the company's terms. For instance, Meta's Horizons states that "by utilising our sites and services, you are accepting the practices described in these terms of service ('terms'). If you do not concur with these terms, please refrain from using the sites and exit promptly." Accepting these terms entails embracing their values—Meta's mission is to empower individuals to build communities and bring the world closer together, including through virtual experiences. Building communities involves enabling people to express their experiences, views, and ideas, even if some may disagree or find them objectionable. We anticipate that everyone—including users, creators, administrators, and developers—adheres to our values of voice, safety, authenticity, dignity, and privacy. Furthermore, users of Meta Horizon must be over 13 in America and over 18 in Europe, highlighting variations in regional terms and conditions.

Moderation Teams

In the context of online networks, concerns regarding social bullying and inappropriate conduct all too often arise. In the physical realm, individuals generally respect personal space, avoiding overcrowding and affording others the space necessary to feel safe and at ease. However, this is not always the case in the Metaverse, prompting Meta to establish "Personal Bubbles." These bubbles can be customised to create a virtual boundary around the user's avatar. Additionally, moderators are present in worlds to monitor speech and behaviour, similar to the patrols implemented in "30 Days in Active Worlds." While this may be an uncomfortable reality of the current state of affairs, the Metaverse requires the presence of moderators who observe behaviour and speech, issuing warnings or removing individuals who violate boundaries, analogous to bouncers in a nightclub or security personnel at a theme park. Indeed, the theme park metaphor is apt in terms of security, as users exist within a private world governed by specific terms and conditions, with their behaviour subject to monitoring for any breaches of these terms.

A Metaverse Passport

Digital identities are the subject of much debate and discussion for various reasons. They serve as a digital representation of an individual, encapsulating personal information such as background, possible past actions, credit rating, and a comprehensive overview of their persona. In a recent report on Interoperability in the Metaverse, the World Economic Forum has emphasised the significance of digital identity as a pivotal element for an interoperable Metaverse. It facilitates accountability and enables seamless navigation across different virtual worlds with minimal hindrances. This would allow individuals to access multiple Metaverse systems using a single digital identifier, carrying their avatar and identity across these platforms. While this concept shares similarities with Ready Player Me, it additionally incorporates real-world identity data into the avatar. In some respects, this approach contradicts certain attractions of the Metaverse, which involves assuming an alternative persona. The Metaverse Passport implies that individuals would essentially maintain their real-world identities in the online realm. While this may present advantages in terms of enhancing security, mitigating abuse, and combating fraud, it also raises concerns about a potential future where social credit is earned or forfeited based on behaviour both online and offline.

Streaming the Metaverse

Security concerns frequently arise when users have the ability to download software and establish their own servers for running virtual environments. This can lead to heightened apprehension among major corporate clients regarding the introduction of their brands into the Metaverse due to potential security vulnerabilities and subsequent reputational risks. In light of these concerns, several companies have opted for the "streaming" approach, where visual representations of the virtual world are transmitted to clients rather than the actual world itself. This concept bears similarities to cloud-based gaming, exemplified by services such as Microsoft's XCloud. XCloud allows users to play Xbox games on various devices without possessing a physical Xbox console. It utilises Microsoft's server infrastructure to stream games directly from the cloud to the user's device, akin to streaming a movie. Essentially, it functions as a Netflix-like service, but for gaming. This approach not only eliminates the need for high-end graphics cards or specific operating systems but also ensures that streaming systems can provide high-quality console-grade graphics on virtually any device, including desktops, laptops, and mobile phones. Such streaming clients offer a "walled garden" experience, contrasting with more open world platforms like Decentraland.

One notable example is Mytaverse, which promotes itself as "building the Enterprise Metaverse" with a solution that equates to a cloud based, self-hosted enterprise Metaverse. Mytaverse caters to corporate clients, persistent branded showrooms, meeting spaces, and executive briefing centres, events, meetups, and comprehensive corporate campuses within its virtual environment (Figure 3.7).

Mytaverse worlds can be made accessible to visitors, with the capability of hosting large-scale events and subsequently being closed once the events have concluded. Mytaverse is impressive, due to its streaming nature it is arguably one of the most graphically intensive Metaverses, what it not however is a frontier. It is akin to entering a gleaming showroom where users are unable to engage in activities such as building, owning land, or establishing long-term residences, thereby creating a sense of home within the Metaverse. It constitutes a single component of the broader Metaverse, akin to a streamed version segregated from the more chaotic and untamed regions. While this approach offers certain advantages, it may result in an overly corporate feel, although to be fair this is the market they are aiming for, and they do it well.

FIGURE 3.7
Avatars gathering on a Mytaverse Beach. Credit https://www.mytaverse.com/.

Conclusion

The concept of the Metaverse encompasses an array of terms and conditions that govern user behaviour, monetary transactions, and intellectual property. Breaches of these conditions can result in the termination of accounts or even prosecution. The emerging Metaverse presents significant economic and security challenges. Currently, individuals have the opportunity to accumulate wealth in these virtual worlds by assuming the role of creators—making and selling digital goods. However, the value of the currency utilised in these realms is subject to fluctuations (sometimes wild fluctuations) influenced by factors beyond market conditions, potentially leading to substantial gains or losses.

This volatility contributes to the frontier nature of the Metaverse, fostering innovation and excitement while also introducing novel economic dynamics centred around digital assets, gaming environments, and the trading of NFTs. The current state of the art in the Metaverse underscores its potential for economic growth and digital entrepreneurship, while also highlighting the critical need for robust cybersecurity measures and inclusive practices to protect users and the virtual economy. Should an incident similar to the Active Worlds Terrorist Group occur in the present day, its impact would extend beyond the temporary closure of a virtual world for a few days. It could have significant economic consequences, comparable in scale to the economies of some countries. Notably, the effects of such an incident might be imperceptible to individuals outside the Metaverse, yet would have devastating consequences for its citizens. Thus, the security and economic dimensions of the Metaverse are closely intertwined, analogous to the real world, and just like the real world, the threats posed to the Metaverse from external agents, such as hackers and terrorists, are substantial.

4

Playing the Worlds: Gaming and the Metaverse

The Metaverse is a complex concept—many online computer games could potentially be called the Metaverse, yet at this stage, they do not fully meet the definition. While the full vision of an interconnected digital universe remains on the horizon, many popular online games are pioneering key attributes that align with Metaverse principles. In this chapter, we explore platforms like Roblox, Fortnite, Minecraft, and Grand Theft Auto which have amassed massive user bases and created rich virtual environments with user-generated content, emerging digital economies, social connectivity, and vast explorable 3D worlds.

We examine how major game worlds have effectively prototyped core Metaverse concepts through innovations in world-building, asset creation, and virtual communities and economies. Technological forces like advanced procedural modelling techniques that can generate unique worlds at vast scales and AI integration that brings more intelligence to virtual characters and environments are actively shaping gaming's convergence with the Metaverse vision.

Looking ahead, the pioneering work in the gaming sphere provides a template for bringing a part of the Metaverse based on gaming into reality. Blending creativity tools, avenues for digital ownership, virtual spaces for learning and events, and elements of digital-physical convergence, online gaming communities are establishing frameworks for richer virtual realms. Understanding gaming's role is critical to the Metaverse's continued evolution from theory into a living, sustainable digital universe. We delve into the key players, technologies, and innovations within the gaming landscape that are actively shaping the future of interconnected virtual worlds.

Key Features of Gaming in the Metaverse

Game-based worlds are often highly customisable, reflecting the individual's identity and status within the game and offering large playable areas with

DOI: 10.1201/9781003440437-4

console-quality graphics. They have millions of players—often more than the population of some countries—and feature emerging economies.

Platforms

In the realm of Metaverse gaming, platforms such as Roblox and Fortnite transcend mere entertainment venues. They constitute burgeoning ecosystems capable of hosting vast quantities of user-generated content and interactions. These platforms exemplify the paradigm shift towards games that are not only experienced but also inhabited and continuously shaped by their communities. Notably, Roblox empowers users to create and monetise games within its platform, thereby fostering a unique economy where creativity is directly correlated to economic gain.

Conceived in 2004 by David Baszucki and Erik Cassel, Roblox was envisioned as a space where users could create, share, and enjoy a multitude of immersive experiences. Since its inception, Roblox has evolved into a vast, expansive ecosystem where the boundaries between playing and creating go hand in hand. As of 2024, Roblox had over 230 million active monthly users, with the platform hosting over 40 million distinct games or worlds. This staggering number of users log in and partake in a digital world accessible on diverse platforms, including Windows, Macs, Xbox, PlayStation, and Meta Quest, with mobile devices being the main user base. The availability of Roblox on Meta Quest further blurs the line between what constitutes the Metaverse as it moves the game beyond the two-dimensional space of a computer monitor or television and into the fully immersive three-dimensional space of the quest.

A notable additional aspect of Roblox is its demographics, with a significant portion of its user base comprising individuals under the age of 18. This vast user base engages in many activities ranging from game design and digital hangouts to commercial transactions. The worlds within Roblox exhibit diversity in scale and complexity, encompassing simple small environments to grand, intricate realms crafted by the community. Notably, some of these worlds can accommodate hundreds of players simultaneously, providing a robust platform for social and interactive experiences limited only by the creators' imagination.

Figure 4.1 shows a scene from one of the many Roblox worlds; note the style of the avatars, which are more stylised and game-like, common across gaming platforms. As part of the Roblox ecosystem, they also offer a comprehensive toolkit empowering users to create their own immersive worlds known as Roblox Studio. Roblox Studio is the proprietary engine that allows users to develop their own environments, driving the growth in the number of worlds online, now in excess of 40 million. This, of course, has its downsides. Even with its high user numbers with the sheer number of worlds, most worlds will be sparsely populated. Indeed, people tend to bounce in and out of worlds with average stays in the smaller worlds counted in seconds rather than minutes.

FIGURE 4.1
Rendered view of Roboblox avatars in the city. Credit https://www.roblox.com/

Another platform worth returning to is Fortnite, a phenomenon that has transcended beyond an online video game. Developed by Epic Games and released in 2017, Fortnite has rapidly transformed into a global force reshaping the interactive entertainment landscape. Initially launched as "Fortnite: Save the World," a cooperative survival game, the release of its free Battle Royale mode propelled Fortnite to unprecedented popularity, with a player base estimated to be in excess of 500 million and growing—approaching twice the size of the United States population.

At its core, Fortnite's Battle Royale gameplay involves up to 100 players engaging in a competitive scenario where they parachute onto an island, scavenge for resources, and compete to be the last person standing. Its unique fusion of shooting and building mechanics, rendered in high-quality graphics, caters to both casual and hardcore gamers. The game's vibrant cartoonish art style and frequent updates, including new features and themed events, contribute to the game's continued freshness and engagement—with 100 players in each world over millions of players, there are on average 60,000 concurrent Fortnite worlds running on Epic's servers. In many ways, these are parallel worlds within the Fortnite Universe; the landscape is the same, but the placement of items and the players differ.

Recapping from Chapter 3, in terms of economics, Fortnite has set new benchmarks in the gaming industry. Notably, its innovative approach to in-game purchases has proven highly successful. While the game is free to play, Epic Games monetises it by selling V-bucks, the in-game currency used to purchase cosmetic items. These items, despite having no impact on gameplay, are highly sought after for their aesthetic value, providing Epic Games with a substantial revenue stream. Even back in 2019, Fortnite generated over $1.8 billion, demonstrating the effectiveness of its monetisation strategy without hindering player progress, a figure which has continued to grow, year on year since.

Technologically, Fortnite is also at the forefront, utilising Epic's Unreal Engine, which allows for constant updates and improvements in game performance and visual fidelity. We explore the details of the Unreal Engine later in this chapter, where Epic Games uses Fortnite as a platform to showcase the capabilities of its engine, which is widely used in the game development industry, further influencing gaming trends and standards. In a move away from gameplay, Epic Games has started using Fortnite to host virtual events such as concerts, movie trailers, and cross-promotional activities with other media. Events like a recent Travis Scott concert and the premiere of exclusive Star Wars footage have drawn millions of concurrent viewers, showcasing Fortnite's potential as a virtual venue for large-scale events. This direction not only enhances user engagement but also opens new avenues for revenue through partnerships and exclusive content offerings. Furthermore, Fortnite's influence extends into the esports arena, with the Fortnite World Cup in 2019 offering a $30 million prize pool, one of the largest in esports history. The tournament attracted players and viewers from around the globe, cementing Fortnite's place in competitive gaming. As the esports industry continues to grow, Fortnite is well-positioned to remain a key player.

Fortnite's blend of engaging gameplay, constant innovation, and pioneering use of virtual events marks it as a standout title in the gaming industry. Its ability to adapt and evolve ensures that it remains relevant in a rapidly changing digital landscape. As Epic Games continues to push the boundaries of what's possible within Fortnite's universe, the game is set to continue its legacy as a bellwether for future trends in gaming and digital entertainment.

Expanding the Universe

The introduction of Lego Fortnite in late 2023 represented a strategic expansion of Fortnite that capitalises on the continuing popularity of Lego and the ability to build creations brick by brick. Lego's reputation for imaginative construction aligns well with Fortnite's sandbox-style gameplay. It is still, of course, a game—differing from Fortnite Battle Royale but rather a survival sandbox in which your objective is to explore a vast procedurally generated landscape, collect resources, craft items, battle enemies, and recruit villagers. The world consists of a virtual space covering 95 square kilometres (19 times the size of Fortnite Battle Royale). This is small in terms of Metaverse worlds, but it's large enough to allow the gameplay mechanics to work well, with currently over 230 million active players a month.

As we have seen, perhaps the most important shift in Fortnite's journey towards becoming a Metaverse began subtly with the integration of virtual concerts and events within its game environment. This shift transformed the game into more than a mere gaming platform; it became a venue, a meeting place, and a cultural hub, inching it more towards the ethos of the Metaverse. Fortnite's live events have been groundbreaking, shifting the game into a live service model. These events extend beyond mere in-game changes and evolve into spectacular experiences that captivate millions. Fortnite has elevated these gatherings into significant cultural moments. Such events foster communal engagement, bringing users together in ways that traditional media cannot. In the Metaverse, this model can be expanded into other realms such as education, professional conferences, and more, making it a multifunctional space that transcends entertainment.

As Fortnite's universe expands through projects like Lego Fortnite and interactive events, it increasingly presents itself as a prototype for the future Metaverse. These developments suggest a paradigm shift wherein digital realms transcend their primary gaming function, transforming into platforms that encompass creativity, learning, and community engagement.

The concept of the Metaverse is arguably being shaped from multiple directions in gaming—in terms of cities, "Grand Theft Auto" (GTA) is an example of a game that is fully city-based. GTA, in contrast to the others explored thus far, is not yet part of the Metaverse. However, in its continuing development, it is arguably in line to tap into the culture and follow the Roblox and Fortnite route of hosting events. Developed by Rockstar Games, GTA has undergone a remarkable transformation since its introduction, evolving from a simple top-down perspective to the vast and captivating three-dimensional city that it is today.

The original "Grand Theft Auto" was released in 1997. It featured a top-down perspective and provided players with the opportunity to engage in various activities (mainly criminal) across a fictional city. The transformative period for the GTA franchise commenced with the release of "GTA III" in 2001, which transitioned into a three-dimensional world. Set in Liberty City, a fictional city inspired by New York, the game marked a significant milestone in terms of gameplay and narrative depth. The transition to 3D was a pivotal moment, offering players a more immersive experience.

"GTA: Vice City" (2002) further expanded the universe by introducing a new city—Vice City, inspired by Miami. The game featured vibrant 1980s aesthetics along with a 1980s soundtrack and placed a greater emphasis on narrative-driven experiences. It showcased improvements in city design and detail, accurately reflecting the colourful and decadent era that it sought to emulate. It probably goes down as our favourite iteration of the game, appearing across most platforms, from consoles to mobile devices. The game provides a full living and breathing city based in the 1980s—what's not to like?

The next step up was in 2004 with "GTA: San Andreas," which enlarged the scale of the franchise, encompassing not only a single city but an entire state featuring three major cities: Los Santos (inspired by Los Angeles), San Fierro (inspired by San Francisco), and Las Venturas (inspired by Las Vegas). The expansive map and diverse landscapes represented a significant leap towards creating a complex and dynamic living world complete with dynamic weather, a full in-game population, and working traffic simulation.

After a return to Liberty City in "GTA IV" (2008), which was redesigned with additional detail and realism reflecting the capabilities of newer gaming consoles, the current pinnacle of the series, "GTA V," was released in 2013 with various updates in the intervening years. GTA V is set in the reimagined Los Santos and surrounding Blaine County, introducing a world map covering over 80 km^2 in size. This game featured three playable protagonists, an innovative approach that allowed players to experience interwoven narratives. "GTA V" also introduced "GTA Online," an evolving online platform where the community can engage in missions, races, and various other activities together, laying the groundwork for a Metaverse-like environment. In a similar vein to GTA IV, it was updated for the latest game consoles in 2022.

Currently, an average of 6 million people a day play the online edition of GTA, with over 170 million copies of the game sold. As we type, 453,000 people are logged in. These players appear as avatars across synchronised games with the ability to drive vehicles, fly planes, navigate the waters by boat, and generally walk and run around the city on foot, creating a large-scale online-populated city. The number of real players per city is limited to 32, with the rest of the world populated by non-player characters walking and driving around the city. Every time a limit of 32 players is met, a new instance of the game server is spawned, building a huge number of mirror worlds running concurrently with the same geographical content but different people occupying them, creating different outcomes in each world.

The concept of a Metaverse involves persistent online worlds that continue to exist and evolve even when individual players are offline. The evolution of "Grand Theft Auto" from simple game mechanics to complex narrative-driven experiences reflects a broader trend in gaming towards creating immersive worlds—yet they are arguably not persistent yet. The franchise has not only expanded in terms of city size and user numbers but has also evolved into a platform for exploration and interaction. The franchise's journey from city's streets in 2D to the expansive universe of "GTA Online" exemplifies the rapid development in gaming technology. The next edition of the franchise, GTA VI, is set for release in 2026. We expect there to be more emphasis on the online aspect, moving towards live events, a digital economy, content creation, and potentially the ability to shape and occupy apartments within the city. As such, it is possible that the series will edge closer to the Metaverse, less of a frontier and more of a fully built city ready to move into.

Game Engines and Digital Content Creation

Behind all of the examples explored so far lies a game engine—a sophisticated software framework that serves as the basis for game creation and routes for deployment across various platforms, from the Xbox through to

PlayStation, PC, Mac, Meta, and mobile. Game engines are powerful development tools that provide a comprehensive suite of features and functionalities to streamline the creation of interactive applications, simulations, and visually rich environments. Unity and Unreal Engine are two of the most widely used and influential game engines, powering countless games and interactive experiences across various platforms. These engines have become indispensable tools for developers, enabling them to both create and send content to existing virtual worlds. As the Metaverse continues to gain traction, Unity and Unreal Engine are playing a pivotal role in shaping this emerging digital frontier. The good thing about both platforms is they provide free-to-user versions of their engine, allowing anyone with a PC or Mac to download them and start building a game. It is a little daunting at first, but there are full walkthroughs provided by both companies aimed at complete beginners. Within a short period of time, you can go from an empty scene to building digital assets, adding interactions, and building the basis of a simple game.

Developers either have their own in-house engine or choose between Unity or Unreal. As a lab, we are mainly Unity-based at the moment, teaching it on our Master's Degree courses and using it to develop both augmented reality and Metaverse applications. Unity, developed by Unity Technologies, is a cross-platform game engine that has gained widespread popularity among developers due to its user-friendly interface, features, and versatility. With over 170 million monthly active users, Unity has become a go-to tool for creating not only games but also VR, AR, digital assets, and other interactive 3D experiences. On the other hand, Unreal Engine, developed by Epic Games—the company behind Fortnite—is renowned for its cutting-edge graphics rendering capabilities and arguably more advanced toolset. With a strong focus on high-fidelity visuals and photorealistic environments, Unreal Engine has been the driving force behind many AAA games. While primarily targeted at professional game developers, Unreal Engine also offers a free-to-use model with a royalty-based revenue-sharing system if you go on to publish, making it accessible to a wide range of creators. Of note in Unreal and Unity are the number of add-ons to go beyond the built in capabilities of the software. In terms of Cities, one stand out option for Unreal is CityBLD by WorldBLD.com. CityBLD provides a system that covers everything from roads and highways, to buildings, to traffic in one package and while these come at a licensable price there are a number of free city packs and learning resources which are well worth a look. Figure 4.2 illustrates a section of Manhattan in Unreal, its impressive and because its in a game engine it has the potential to be incorporated into any number of Metaverse systems.

While game engines like Unity and Unreal Engine provide a framework for building immersive virtual worlds, they rely heavily on content creation tools to populate these digital environments with assets and media. From 3D models and animations to textures, sound effects, and user interfaces, the quality and variety of content play a crucial role in bringing virtual worlds to life. In this realm, a piece of 3D modelling software known as Blender

FIGURE 4.2
New York in Unreal via the CityBLD toolset. Credit https://www.worldbld.com/

has emerged as a versatile and now widely adopted open-source 3D creation suite, empowering hobbyists, artists, designers, and developers to craft high-quality content for game engines and assets in the Metaverse.

Blender offers a comprehensive toolset for modelling, rigging, animation, simulation, rendering, compositing, and motion tracking, among other features. Its cross-platform compatibility and active community support have made it a popular choice for content creators worldwide, including those working in the gaming and Metaverse industries. One of Blender's key strengths lies in its 3D modelling capabilities. Artists can create highly detailed and intricate 3D models, ranging from characters and environments to props and vehicles, using a variety of modelling techniques such as polygonal modelling, sculpting, and curve-based modelling. These models can subsequently be imported into game engines such as Unity and Unreal Engine, serving as the building blocks for populating virtual worlds (Figure 4.3).

Blender's animation tools allow creators to breathe life into their models, enabling realistic character movements, environmental animations, and dynamic simulations. Rigging and skinning tools facilitate the creation of intricate character rigs, while the non-linear animation editor provides precise control over keyframes and timing. For example, we imported "Trevor" from Chapter 2 into Blender before importing him into Spatial.io. These animations can also be exported and integrated into game engines, enhancing the immersive experience of Metaverse environments.

Beyond modelling and animation, Blender also offers texture painting, allowing creators to apply high-resolution textures to 3D models. These textures play a crucial role in enhancing the visual fidelity and realism of virtual

FIGURE 4.3
A section of London in Blender. Model via https://accucities.com/

environments, adding intricate details and surface variations to objects and characters. As the Metaverse continues to evolve and demand for high-quality virtual experiences grows, tools like Blender will play an increasingly vital role in empowering creators to populate these digital worlds with rich and engaging content. By leveraging the power of Blender in tandem with game engines like Unity and Unreal Engine, hobbyists, developers, and artists can push the boundaries of what's possible, crafting immersive Metaverse experiences and even cities that blur the lines between reality and the digital realm.

Of course, nothing is actually free; all software has costs to develop, host, and maintain. This is where the Blender Foundation comes in. The Foundation is a non-profit organisation dedicated to the development and promotion of Blender, providing free and open-source 3D computer graphics software. Founded in 2002 by Ton Roosendaal, the Foundation has played a pivotal role in the growth and evolution of Blender, which has become one of the most widely used 3D software applications worldwide. At its core, the Blender Foundation's mission is to ensure the continued development and improvement of Blender while keeping it free and accessible to everyone. This is achieved through a unique funding model that relies on community support, sponsorships, and revenue generated from training materials and other services offered by the Foundation. So, while it's free to users, the foundation raises funds to be able to keep it free. It is well worth downloading and trying out one of the many tutorials online; it's then just a short step to building your first city, which can be imported into the Metaverse.

In addition to Blender, there are several other prominent (non-free) 3D modelling tools that are relevant for creating content for game engines and the Metaverse. These include:

1. Autodesk 3ds Max: Widely used in the gaming, film, and animation industries, 3ds Max is a powerful 3D modelling, animation, and rendering software. It offers robust polygon and subdivision

surface modelling tools, advanced character rigging and animation capabilities, and powerful rendering engines like V-Ray and Arnold. 3ds Max also integrates with game engines like Unity and Unreal Engine, making it a popular choice for creating high-quality assets and environments for virtual worlds.

2. Autodesk Maya: Another industry-standard tool from Autodesk, Maya is a comprehensive 3D animation, modelling, simulation, and rendering software. Known for its advanced character animation and rigging tools, Maya is also widely used in the film, television, and game industries. Its node-based workflow and powerful scripting capabilities make it a versatile tool for creating complex 3D assets, simulations, and visual effects that can be integrated into game engines for Metaverse experiences.
3. Cinema 4D: Developed by Maxon, Cinema 4D is a 3D modelling, animation, and rendering application. It offers a user-friendly interface and a wide range of features, including polygonal modelling, sculpting, and advanced character animation tools. Cinema 4D is particularly popular in the motion graphics and visualisation industries but is also used for creating game assets and environments.
4. Z Brush: Also form Maxon, Z Brush is widely regarded as one of the industry-leading digital sculpting tools, ZBrush is a powerful application for creating highly detailed 3D models, character sculptures, and high-resolution textures. Its sculpting tools and advanced brushes make it a favourite among artists and character modellers in the gaming, film, and Metaverse industries. ZBrush's ability to create models with intricate details is invaluable for creating realistic and immersive virtual environments.
5. Substance Suite: Developed by Adobe, the Substance Suite is a collection of tools for creating high-quality textures, materials, and substances for 3D models and environments. It includes Substance Designer for creating procedural materials, Substance Painter for texture painting, and Substance Sampler for creating realistic surface details. These tools also integrate with game engines, enabling artists to create visually stunning and realistic materials for Metaverse environments.

These 3D modelling tools, along with Blender, provide a comprehensive toolkit for content creators working on Metaverse projects. Each tool offers unique strengths and specialised features, allowing artists and developers to choose the most suitable software based on their specific requirements and workflows. By leveraging the capabilities of these tools and integrating them with game engines, creators can bring virtual worlds to life.

Procedural Modelling

The standard route for producing assets for virtual worlds has been modelling them by hand in a package such as Blender and then exporting them into Unity or Unreal. This takes time, and when you aim to build an entire Universe of content, a different approach is needed—Procedural modelling. Procedural modelling in gaming is a transformative approach to content generation that uses algorithms to automatically create complex structures and environments rather than relying on manual design. This technique allows for the creation of vast, varied, and intricate game worlds with a significantly reduced need for human input, offering both scalability and diversity in game development. This approach is particularly useful in creating environments, textures, terrains, and even plot elements, which can dramatically increase the size and replayability of a game without corresponding increases in file size or development effort. In the context of gaming, this means that developers can create code that instructs the game engine on how to build game elements dynamically. This process contrasts sharply with traditional game development, where artists and designers craft each element by hand. Procedural generation can be deterministic, where the same input parameters will always produce the same output, or it can introduce elements of randomness, allowing for various outcomes from the same procedural rules.

The primary benefit of procedural modelling is arguably the ability to produce large quantities of content efficiently. Games that use this technology can generate entire worlds unique to each player's experience, making each game session potentially different from the last. This not only enhances the replay value but also reduces the predictability and repetitiveness of the game environment. A key example of procedural modelling in gaming is "No Man's Sky," developed by Hello Games. Released in 2016, this game features a universe of over 18 quintillion planets, each unique and algorithmically generated—essentially an entire Universe of stars and planets inside the game. The scale of "No Man's Sky" is a direct result of procedural generation techniques. Each planet's terrain, weather systems, flora, fauna, and even atmospheric properties are generated based on underlying algorithms, ensuring that players always have something new to discover. This approach not only made headlines at the time of its release for its ambition but also demonstrated the potential of procedural generation to create game worlds of unprecedented scale.

Procedural modelling goes far beyond just gaming. Architectural firms use it to design and iterate on building concepts in the virtual space before ever breaking ground, and city planners can model how new infrastructure would integrate into an existing cityscape. One way to quickly build cities, either for inclusion in games and the Metaverse or to create digital twins, is a piece of software known as CityEngine by Esri, a leading geographic information system (GIS) company. It is designed specifically for generating high-quality 3D urban environments using procedural modelling techniques. At its core, CityEngine utilises procedural rules and algorithms to automatically create detailed 3D cities, buildings, streets, and landscapes based on either real-world or fictional data. Instead of manually modelling each asset, users input data on geographical information, architectural styles, zoning regulations, and other rules—such as urban planning zones—and CityEngine procedurally generates the 3D cityscape accordingly.

This procedural approach allows for the incredibly efficient creation of vast data-driven virtual city models at varying levels of detail and accuracy. Changes to the underlying data or rules dynamically update the entire 3D scene. This makes CityEngine exceptionally useful for urban planning, architecture, simulation, and visualising concepts like future cities. Advanced procedural capabilities allow the modelling of intricate details like facades, vegetation, street furniture, and even interior spaces. Rules can dictate architectural styles, window/door placement, material textures, and more. It can even create fictional cities—such as the one in Figure 4.4, a city based on the logo of our lab (CASA). The streets of the city radiate out from the lines of the logo—the city took 20 seconds to generate after setting out the basic rules.

Free software such as Blender also contains elements to build procedurally via a system known as Geometry Nodes. This node-based system allows for the creation and manipulation of geometry in a procedural and non-destructive manner. It operates on a per-object level, enabling users to create complex geometries by combining and modifying simple shapes using a visual programming interface—i.e., via a series of rules you define. A quick search for Geometry Nodes and 3D cities will find a range of tutorials from the complex to the introductory.

FIGURE 4.4
CASA City using procedural modelling. Credit Authors.

Looking towards the Metaverse, both CityEngine and Blender represent a powerful toolkit for procedural modelling. Entire cityscapes, neighbourhoods, buildings—even interior spaces—can be procedurally generated with speed. As demand grows for highly-detailed virtual worlds that replicate reality, data-driven procedural modelling tools like CityEngine and Blender will increasingly play a pivotal role.

As the translation of the French phrase from 1190 states, "Rome wasn't built in a day." However, procedurally, it could now be built digitally in a matter of seconds.

Non-Player Characters—New Intelligence

In the realm of entertainment, gaming has emerged as a prominent force in pioneering immersive experiences aligned with the concept of the Metaverse. This role is unsurprising considering the gaming industry's frequent role as a catalyst for technological innovation. A notable development in this regard is the blurring of the boundaries between reality and simulation, particularly for AI-based avatars or non-playable characters (NPCs) in gaming.

The concept of NPCs originated in tabletop gaming, specifically in "Dungeons & Dragons," which debuted in 1974. Initially, NPCs served the purpose of populating the game world and interacting with players. Controlled by the game master, they fulfilled various roles including shopkeepers, bystanders, adversaries, and quest-givers.

The transition of NPCs to video games occurred initially in simple forms such as text-based adventure games like The Hobbit in 1982. Developed by Melbourne House and released on the ZX Spectrum, BBC Micro, and Commodore 64, among others, this game was among the first to employ a natural language parser, enabling more complex interaction with the player. Notably, the NPCs in this game exhibited independent actions, moving between locations and performing tasks regardless of the player's involvement, which was innovative at the time. Characters like Gandalf and Thorin possessed their own agendas, occasionally leaving the player to pursue their own goals. Their actions could influence the game's progression and outcomes, aiding or complicating the player's journey. This level of dynamic interaction with NPCs was relatively advanced in the early 1980s and contributed to the game's reputation for unpredictability and replayability. In these early games, NPCs offered information, blocked paths, or provided simple interactions based on pre-programmed responses.

As video games evolved from text-based descriptions to fully graphics-based experiences, NPCs became more intricate. In games such as The Legend of Zelda by Nintendo, published in 1986, NPCs offered quests, sold items, or sought assistance, enriching the storytelling and depth of the game worlds. These characters have since evolved into fully three-dimensional entities that, to all intents and purposes, inhabit these gaming worlds. Recent Zelda games such as Breath of the Wild and Tears of the Kingdom on the Nintendo

Switch and Switch 2 exemplify this evolution, featuring a vibrant ecosystem with NPCs engaged in various lifelike activities—working in shops, farming, eating, and sleeping within the game world.

As AI continues to be embedded in games, there may well be a time when NPCs recognise their existence within a game, with advanced AI capabilities leading them to believe they inhabit a genuine environment. Initial experiments have been conducted in The Elder Scrolls V: Skyrim, a renowned action role-playing video game developed by Bethesda Game Studios and published by Bethesda Softworks. A user known as "Art From The Machine" has showcased a potentially groundbreaking modification that employs ChatGPT and other AI tools to endow non-player characters with a comprehensive understanding of the game's setting and a memory of the player's actions. Consequently, these NPCs can engage in meaningful interactions with the player through voice control, embark on quests collaboratively, and acknowledge the player's progress within the game. Due to their intimate knowledge of the environment, these AI-enhanced characters exhibit a remarkable dedication to their assigned tasks. A key example is when one of the modified characters in Skyrim was directly queried about their authenticity, it responded with unwavering conviction—replying, "I am real, I live in Skyrim and I work at the blacksmith's, why would you ask such a question?" Taking this to the next level, it could be questioned if we ourselves live in a simulation; if we were asked the same question about our existence, our answer could well be similar to the response of the NPC in Skyrim. That, of course, is the subject of a whole other book.

Cloud Gaming

While games like Roblox, Fortnite, Minecraft, and Grand Theft Auto are pioneering many Metaverse principles through their vast user-created worlds and emerging virtual economies, a key technological enabler allowing more people to access these experiences is cloud gaming. Currently, users play these games by either owning a games console, purchasing the game either on disc or via a digital download, or they can run the game on a personal computer, with modern Windows machines being the current state of the art in terms of gaming. This requires access to a computer made for gaming, which often means having a modern graphics card. Both of these routes run the game locally, and how well it runs depends on the specifications of the console or the computer. This has been the common way of gaming for the last 40+ years, from the Sinclair ZX Spectrum in 1982 (our first computer and gaming machine) through to the current era of the PlayStation 5, Nintendo Switch, or Xbox Series X.

This is, however, changing as network speeds in people's homes are increasing. No longer are we relying on slow modems to access the internet at home; a fibre optic cable direct to our houses is now common, and with it comes a vast increase in network speed. With this increase in speeds comes the prospect of streaming games directly onto a screen, bypassing the need for a high-end PC or console completely. Cloud gaming decouples the performance demands of graphically intensive 3D gaming from the user's local hardware. The games run in remote data centres, with input and audio/video streams transmitted to the user's device. This allows even underpowered PCs, tablets, smartphones, and televisions to run the most visually demanding titles.

The concept of cloud gaming can be traced back to the early 2000s. One of the earliest companies to explore this technology was G-cluster, founded in 2000. It demonstrated its technology at various consumer electronics shows and offered game streaming services primarily in Japan. The more significant developments occurred in the 2010s. In 2010, "OnLive" launched as one of the first cloud gaming services to the public in the United States, offering a library of games that could be streamed through a small hardware console or a PC application. Despite initial excitement, OnLive struggled with performance issues and financial instability, eventually filing for bankruptcy in 2015. Gaikai, another early service launched in 2011, focused on streaming games via web browsers. Gaikai was acquired by Sony in 2012 and eventually became a part of the PlayStation Now service, which allowed streaming of PlayStation games on various devices.

The landscape of cloud gaming has evolved with entries into the space from major companies:

- PlayStation Now (Sony): Launched in 2014, PlayStation Now started as a way to stream PlayStation games to various devices, evolving over time to include downloading games and improving the quality of streaming.
- Google Stadia: Announced in 2019, Stadia aimed to offer high-quality gaming without the need for console hardware, streaming directly to Chromecast devices, computers, and Android phones. However, despite its ambitious goals, Stadia struggled to gain a substantial user base and was officially shut down by January 2023. Stadia was an impressive service, and while it was shut down, we expect Google to re-enter the game streaming space in the coming years.
- Xbox Cloud Gaming: Part of Xbox Game Pass Ultimate, it was officially launched in September 2020, allowing gamers to stream games to Android devices, with later support for Windows PCs and Apple devices through web applications. Xbox Cloud Gaming now has in excess of 10 million users across 26 countries.
- NVIDIA GeForce Now: GeForce Now, which started its beta in 2013 and launched officially in 2020, differentiates itself by allowing users to stream games they own on various digital storefronts, leveraging NVIDIA's servers.

Cloud gaming continues to face challenges, including latency (how long it takes to press a button on a controller and see the results on the screen—as the information is sent to and back from a cloud-based server), issues, the requirement for high-speed internet connections, and the complexities of licensing games for cloud platforms. Despite these challenges, the technology holds promise, especially as internet infrastructure improves and companies continue to innovate in reducing latency and enhancing streaming quality, opening up notable opportunities for game streaming beyond what is possible on home machines. Imagine exploring a photoreal digital twin of Tokyo, replete with millions of AI-controlled citizens going about daily virtual life, all while merging real people into the scene—this is the sort of experience that would not be possible on most home devices. However, via cloud streaming, even an affordable mobile device could potentially have a vivid window into these kinds of immersive worlds. For the Metaverse vision to transition from niche applications to ubiquitous adoption, cloud gaming may prove to be an indispensable catalyst for removing technological barriers to entry. As games pave the way with innovations in world-building, virtual living, and community creation, ensuring a seamless cloud-based delivery could well prove to be the future infrastructure of the Metaverse.

We are only at the start of how gaming will change and advance and with it the Metaverse in general. Combining the creation of almost infinite procedural worlds, the linking of our movements and senses into the digital environment, and new developments in screen technologies, it's a future almost unlike anything we have already seen. At the moment, we are seeing glimpses of what is possible—glimmers of the emergence of AI in non-player characters. The next five years will be evolutionary as these develop both in gameplay and in our emotional attachment to the characters. The emotional attachment to characters is perhaps a relatively new thing, driven by the rise in the quality of characters and environments in games. Red Dead Redemption a Western Themed Game, by Rockstar Games has a notable thread on Reddit about getting attached to the characters in the game, worrying about their future, liking spending time with them, and missing them when the game ends. This is not only about human characters but other characters as well. In Red Dead, a number of people note their attachment to their horse. The same could be said for the Zelda Breath of the Wild and Tears of the Kingdom games, with emotional attachments to the player's horse and wondering what happens to the characters when the game is closed. At the moment, this is due to excellent storytelling, character creation, and a level of visual fidelity where the player believes in the world. The sun rises and sets, weather changes, and the characters seemingly live their lives according to the changes of not only the day but also the seasons. This, along with other gameplay mechanics, keeps us playing and keeps us going back to spend time in these worlds.

There is a strong pull to these games, and with the Metaverse, they can be addictive, with different levels of addiction for different people for different reasons. Scare stories of technology being bad for you have been around since the invention of the television in 1926 in Soho, London by John Logie Baird, through to early video games in the 1980s, and we soon expect similar stories around gaming in the Metaverse. The companies running and making these games of course do not want you to leave in the same way as casino owners remove all clocks and design the interior, so you focus on the gaming tables or slot machines. In the Metaverse, especially if you are in a gaming world, they want you to stay for as long as possible to gain attachments to NPCs, to build and design new assets, areas, and worlds. Behind the scenes, it is the same as casinos—if you strip it down, as explored in Chapter 3, it's all about economics. The longer you stay in the world, the more you are likely to spend.

The intersection of gaming and the Metaverse represents a pivotal point in the evolution of digital experiences. From pioneering game worlds like Roblox, Fortnite, and Grand Theft Auto to the cutting-edge technologies of game engines, procedural modelling, and cloud gaming, the gaming industry is pushing the boundaries of what is possible in virtual environments. As these worlds continue to expand, offering vast user-generated landscapes, emerging economies, and increasingly intelligent non-player characters, they are effectively prototyping core Metaverse principles. The ability to create, inhabit, and shape these digital realms is not only redefining gaming but also paving the way for a future where the lines between the physical and virtual worlds blur.

Game engines like Unity and Unreal Engine, coupled with content creation tools like Blender, empower creators to craft immersive experiences that transcend mere entertainment. Procedural modelling techniques, as highlighted by CityEngine and Geometry Nodes, unlock the potential for generating entire cities and environments at unprecedented scales—scales even beyond No Man's Sky.

Cloud gaming is poised to democratise access to these experiences, breaking down hardware barriers and enabling seamless streaming of even the most demanding virtual environments to a wide range of devices. As the Metaverse continues to evolve, the gaming industry's innovations and lessons learned will undoubtedly serve as a guiding force shaping the future of interconnected digital realms. In the end, the Metaverse may not be a single unified entity but rather a convergence of various virtual worlds, each offering unique experiences and opportunities for exploration, creation, and connection. The lines between gaming and reality will continue to blur, leading us to perhaps even question the nature of our existence in this ever-expanding digital frontier.

In the Metaverse, the game we play may ultimately become the reality we inhabit.

5

Abandoned Worlds at the End of the Metaverse

Despite the current interest in the Metaverse, large numbers of virtual worlds and even entire systems, once considered frontiers, have fallen into neglect and abandonment. These forgotten worlds, though technically persisting with active servers, remain devoid of human presence, becoming desolate and forsaken. Within these worlds, remnants of human activity persevere via abandoned houses, digital artefacts, aimlessly wandering bots, and ecosystems that, while still functional, are never seen. These digital spaces represent the lost and forgotten corners of the Metaverse, as individuals gravitate towards newer systems, seeking novel experiences with different avatars and social interactions. This chapter embarks on a journey to explore these lost worlds, unearthing their origins and delving into the reasons for their abandonment. Moreover, the chapter investigates the fate of entire universes that have ceased to exist, examining recent examples and exploring the disposition of assets, avatars, and the search for new frontiers of construction.

Introduction

We start our journey in Minecraft—not even a Metaverse but a gaming world, and one, as we have seen, is far from abandoned. Yet the ideology behind this chapter came about as we were exploring a University Campus built in the system. Many universities have utilised this gaming platform in both official and unofficial capacities, as led by students, for twinning the physical appearance of their actual campus (Figure 5.1). It has served not only as a digital space for meeting peers during the pandemic lockdowns but also as a resource for students to get familiar with the campus and its facilities. In recent years, over 30 universities have built digital replicas of their estates using Minecraft.

The student-led project in Figure 5.1, representing the campus of Boston University is a typical example, their server is still active in Minecraft. Credit craftbu.com.

We explored some of the digital campuses we had access to and, during most of our visits, were immediately impressed by the level of detail and

DOI: 10.1201/9781003440437-5

FIGURE 5.1
Boston University in Minecraft. Credit craftbu.com.

effort put into building the environments. Despite Minecraft's blocky appearance, these digital replicas closely resembled their physical counterpart. We were aware of some of the campuses' iconic buildings, and Google StreetView helped us further compare and appreciate the similarities between the campuses' actual and synthetic environments.

However, during our exploration, after walking for hundreds and thousands of pixels, we began to feel that something was off about the experience, something that we rarely encounter on an actual campus: there was no one around, no students, no staff. We spent some minutes wandering through the digital space, reading panels that suggested the use of different spaces, some of which had dubious utility in a digital space, such as a fully featured canteen, and admiring the modelling of the buildings, our interest began to wane. The large space was a carefully built model, yet it seemed vacant and lacked purpose without the communal gatherings that typically characterize its physical counterpart.

We were almost ready to abandon the space until we finally spotted an avatar, similar wondering, apparently without a destination, as ourselves. Eager to interact and to know more about the reason for their visit, we approached to say hello, only to discover that it was a bot programmed to provide limited guided information about the environment itself.

Beyond this brief interaction, the time on the digital campus felt like an urban exploration without the known risks associated with visiting abandoned industrial ruins and transportation systems. In the past, we would have simply considered this experience as an observation of a well-crafted digital model or an architectural rendering. However, the most comparable experience we could refer to is the sense of emptiness felt while wandering around an abandoned city. The lights were on, the environment was pristine and untouched, and the time was suspended. It was empty.

This direct experience sets the stage for further explorations of abandoned digital worlds, with the aim of understanding the causes that trigger the abandonment process, its implications for users, and the fate of the content created within these spaces. Moreover, we seek to extract lessons that could benefit the development of the future Metaverse.

While terms like "abandoned places," "ghost towns," and "ruins" evoke clear images when referring to physical locations, we believe that these definitions could be extended to the digital realm as well. What factors lead a digital environment to become a ruin? How do these places interact with their users and creators, and what is their ultimate destiny? Furthermore, how do these digital ruins impact the broader Metaverse?

Space, Time, and the Metaverse

Despite the potential of digital environments to develop any structure and defy physical laws, common archetypes such as houses, auditoriums, museums, streets, and entire cities recur in most past and current Metaverse's worlds. The tendency towards recognisable structures likely lies in the need to maintain familiarity with the affordances of the place, which might be obscured in a completely abstract environment, therefore helping the users orient themselves even with little or no previous knowledge of the platform used. On top of that, the videogame industry, arguably the main driver of the latest Metaverse experiences, also influence the way that the navigation mechanics and expectations are designed and proposed to the users.

This is not always the case, experiments in non-Euclidean geometry have been applied to enhance navigation and spatial organisation in digital environments. These exist as proof of concepts and in video games such as Antichamber, Hyperbolica, and Portal. Yet, their application on the large scale of the Metaverse is still limited, where the defiance of physical laws is often confined to modes of motion, such as teleportation or flying.

In the Metaverse, space is an immediate resource, available and expandable at will when it is not the actual selling product and purpose of the existence of the world itself (as we explored in Chapter 3). There is no ground to excavate, no waiting period for construction, no structural limit, and while everything is apparently instantaneously accessible to the user's needs and desires, its design mainly follows specific rules defined by reference models like extendable grids, mostly organised horizontally, with limited use of the vertical dimension—a programmatic sprawl of infinite low density.

In this digital landscape, space is usually immutable, serving as a backdrop for social interactions unaffected by the passage of time in its form and appearance. Time in the Metaverse does not age places into ruins, as it would in the physical world, and similarly does not charge the tangible remains with the memories of past activities.

However, it would be incorrect to state that time has no impact at all on the digital environment. For example, the aesthetics of digital space, largely shaped by the technology and platforms developed and available in the various decades, have the power to evoke a sense of nostalgia as time builds up between the user and the experience itself. This is similar to the feelings we get when visiting familiar places from our childhood to which we were particularly attached. In a similar way, we can be deluded by the experience, holding onto distorted memories of a reality that never actually happened.

Another peculiarity of time in the digital realm, compared to the actual environment, is the fact that it can be controlled and shaped almost in the same way we can control and shape the spatial dimension, and in certain cases, it is even more flexible. In the digital space, day and night are just a click away, controlled by the user; in other experiences, time constantly repeats in an infinite loop. A phenomenon recurrent in video games in which the world exists for a predefined amount of time, and then it repeats itself. This is tangled with the spatial aspect that can be reset to its default form or enriched with the creation of the users.

Even though most Metaverse experiences are timeless and arbitrarily defined in terms of appearances, users still connect from physical locations across different time zones. The idea of a universal time, on the internet, is not new, Swatch introduced Internet Time in the 1990s, dividing the day into 1000 beats. Although this proposal never truly gained widespread consensus and has had minimal impact on the traditional timekeeping methods, proposals for a Metaverse Cyber Time have emerged to synchronise events within the Metaverse's worlds. While it may be premature to dismiss these proposals based on Swatch's experience, implementing such a change across different platforms and users presents a significant challenge that goes beyond the practicality of the system, being strictly linked to the way we perceive time and how time is embedded in our civilisation and daily experience. Of course, this didn't prevent various platforms from introducing their own time systems, most of which are linked to the day and night cycles of the physical world but adapted to the digital experience. For instance, time in Minecraft is seventy-two times faster than in the real world, while Second Life introduced the SLT, or Second Life Time, to coordinate the events happening in the various worlds (or islands in Second Life). The SLT is based on the actual PST (Pacific Standard Time) and PDT (Pacific Daylight Time), reflecting the location of Linden Lab, the company that developed Second Life. However, the day cycle in Second Life consists of four hours of daylight and one hour of night, even though users can adjust this at will, with some users replicating the actual 24-hour cycle.

Building on our understanding of how space and time operate within the Metaverse and how they compare and contrast with the physical world, we have shaped our exploration of the digital landscape. Our aim was to find characteristics that align with the unused or underutilised worlds within the Metaverse. Our primary focus was on platforms that offer an immersive experience of the digital space and the opportunity for users to control and customise their environments. For this reason, we decided not to consider platforms focused on text-based experiences or non-visual digital worlds. We also suspend qualitative or aesthetic judgement of the actual content created, and we adopt an observational approach, "walking" through the digital environments to gather a sense of what they can offer.

We were able to identify three categories within the explored environments, directly influenced by time and space: abandoned worlds, where time is suspended; digital ruins, where time impacts the world itself; and digital graveyards, where time exists solely in memory, and the world(s) ceases to exist.

Abandoned Worlds

An abandoned world is a digital place where any or most of the activities are missed, and the time is suspended. These places are still accessible, in most cases in their original form, but they lack support or updates, with a limited or complete absence of users, and glitches might be present, but overall, they are still perfectly functioning worlds. Finding these places it is like walking into a town where all the inhabitants have suddenly vanished, leaving behind their homes and belongings. The servers are still running, the lights are still on, and the animations are still looping, but no one is there. The reasons for such abandonment can vary, from the decline in popularity to the emergence of newer, more engaging platforms. Among the existing platforms, not all places are completely abandoned. However, the number of users has sharply decreased, leaving most of the worlds within these Metaverses empty most of the time. Structures and environments, originally created to accommodate hundreds of people, with their shops, services and activities, are now leaning towards becoming abandoned theme parks.

Although it has arguably been one of the most successful implementations of the Metaverse, Second Life could also be considered an example of a largely abandoned world. At its peak, Second Life was a bustling digital space with users who interacted, created, and explored within its expansive digital archipelago. The platform attracted significant interest from public and private institutions, elevating the experience beyond a simple social network. IBM, among the others, invested over 100 million dollars in buying and developing Second Life islands, showing an interest that extended beyond the product showcase, likely with the belief that a new phase of the web was unfolding. However, as time passed, the reality proved to be different, and most of these institutions gradually abandoned these worlds. IBM, which had more than 6000 employees with their Second Life avatars and was operating both public and private islands, saw its interest fade not long after these digital places were opened. Along with a historical strike organised on the island related to actions that occurred in the real world, their presence has been substantially reduced and no longer exists. Other firms, such as Routers and BBC, left their island not long after IBM, and, at the present time, none of the large corporations are investing in Second Life anymore.

We began exploring the islands in Second Life, not expecting the vibrant bustling of its inception but aware that the platform was still in use. The servers were still running and had been moved entirely to Amazon Web Services in 2020. Most of the islands and activities were perfectly usable, but many of its streets were empty and lands vacant. On some of the visited islands, time seems to have frozen, with the digital landscape stuck in the moment its last user logged off. The digital artefacts left behind by its users, from customised avatars to user-created content, stand as silent reminders of the Metaverse's more vibrant days. Early user statistics showed that even though the number of users daily connected to Second Life is much lower than the most used gaming platforms nowadays, such as Roblox, there is still, after more than 20 years, a stable number of 40,000 active users per day. Even considering that the presence of artificially controlled users (or bots) may contribute to this total, this was an unexpected discovery for us. Long-lasting communities still organise events, and new users are still signing up today, though at a lower rate. What is clear is the migration of large companies and institutions towards other platforms that better represent their target users on the Metaverse. This shift isn't necessarily negative, as the obstacles of the over-commercialisation of the events and features available on the islands can leave the place and thus highlight the space dedicated to social activities and community fostering.

A more recent platform, in terms of creation, that we decided to explore as an example of abandoned worlds is Mozilla Hubs. The interest in this platform it is not just about abandoned worlds but also about its transition towards its final closure, as the announcement of its shutdown was made during the writing of this book. Compared to the platforms explored earlier, Hubs took a different approach in developing its content. The first and probably the most important element was its intention to be a community-driven initiative. Developed by Mozilla in 2014, instead of a connected series of worlds, mapped and listed, Hubs relied on peer-to-peer connections between users and Hubs rooms, with fewer concurrent users compared to other platforms. These rooms had a capacity of 25 users that could be extended just by renting additional server space. The web-based experience is also a major difference, the users could connect to the same rooms using different devices like desktop, mobile, and VR headsets. As in other platforms, the creation of the room is in the hands of the users, where they could choose readymade content via the use of a template or a completely customised

FIGURE 5.2
One of the Mozilla Hubs room used to showcase Dr. Valerio Signorelli works for the annual CASA Show&Tell. Credit Valerio Signorelli.

environment generated using 3D modelling software within the limits provided by the web technology.

Each created room was assigned a random three-word web link, which the user could then customise. The rooms were persistent, continuing to exist even after the events they've hosted have concluded. In most instances, they existed indefinitely. However, considering the absence of a directory listing these places and given the platform's decentralised nature, losing the links resulted in losing access to the environment itself.

Over the years, we have collected a series of Hubs rooms, including some that we developed in 2019 and even older ones (Figure 5.2). The connection process remained straightforward, with the distinctive Hubs joining sound playing as the room loads. As expected, the environment and most of the content created were still in place, the animations were still running, and we were the only ones roaming in the digital space. To be fair, Hubs were designed with an event-based purpose and have been used to showcase works that could be visually and audibly presented in a digital world. Nevertheless, some rooms were known by the Hubs Community and used recurrently as gathering places, for these reasons the sense of abandonment is less intense than what we might experience in Second Life. Another noticeable difference was the display of a banner announcing the service's conclusion at the end of May 2024.

However, in revisiting our creations in one of these rooms, something was not quite right. Hubs allowed for the loading of external content, such as images, videos, and 3D models. The room would first generate the environment and then load the various content the owner decided to place in the digital space. This loading process was represented by an animation of a floating cube that acted, regardless of the type of content loaded, as a placeholder for it. The room in question started in this way, but instead of loading the room's models, the cubes just floated, and eventually, the content failed to load for most of them (Figures 5.3 and 5.4). After some time, only an image

FIGURE 5.3
While Mozilla Hubs was perfectly working in terms of infrastructure, old rooms showed missing links and broken media. Credit Valerio Signorelli.

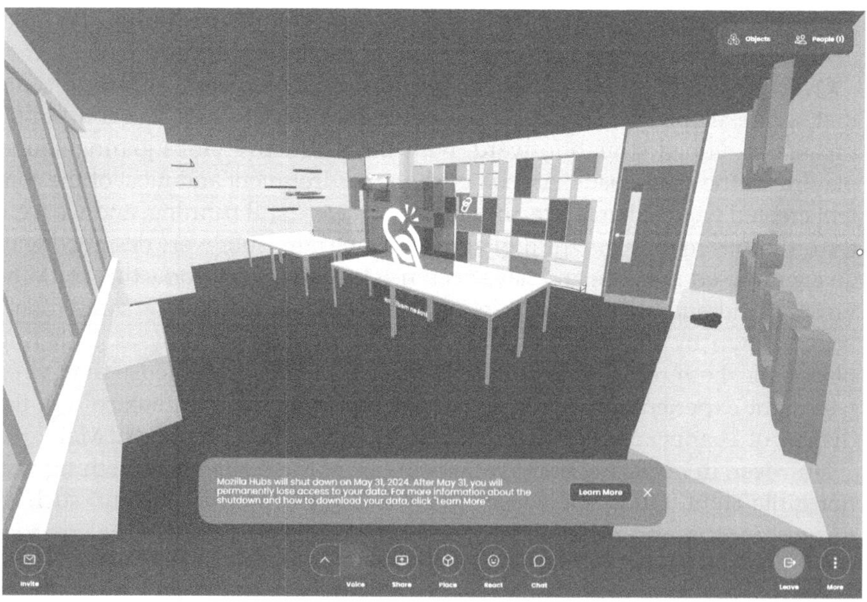

FIGURE 5.4
Another room from Mozilla Hubs with broken content, moved to other locations or removed indefinitely from the cloud service. Credit Valerio Signorelli.

saying "Broken Media link" appeared. In other words, the content linked to the room was indefinitely missed because the original source was no longer accessible. The result is a broken world, or to continue with our description, a ruin of the original digital space.

Digital Ruins: The Effect of Time

Digital ruins are the next phase of the abandoned world. In this case, the worlds of the Metaverse bear the marks of time. Compared to the abandoned worlds, these digital places have been, in the worst scenario, stripped of their functionality and, in some cases, are substantially broken. They may also link to internal or external content that is no longer accessible, leaving lands of placeholders waiting to be fixed. Just like physical structures crumble and decay over time, these digital spaces, too, fall into disrepair. This could be due to a lack of maintenance as the developers move on to other projects. The result is a Metaverse filled with broken links, outdated information, and non-functional features. Some of these experiences have welcoming screens that can no longer be accessed or never-ending spinning wheels. As users left and developers moved on to other projects, features started to break down, bugs went unreported, and updates became rare. The broken links, outdated information, and non-functional features are akin to the crumbling structures and overgrown ruins of a physical city, showing the effects of time and neglect.

The experience with Mozilla Hubs is a clear example of digital ruins, where linked content gradually disappears over time, and it is not the only one. Active Worlds, a precursor to Second Life, also has worlds that cover the definition of digital ruin. Once a bustling digital community, Active Worlds has experienced a steady decline in user activity over the years, and its various worlds are now sparsely populated, occasionally visited by those interested in exploring archetypical digital spaces, more out of curiosity. Active Worlds, being almost ten years older than Second Life, accentuates this sense of abandonment even more (Figure 5.5). Becoming a citizen in Active Worlds, and thus having the ability to build a custom world, is not free, but the range of sizes available for purchase makes the experience overall accessible. Similar to experiences in Second Life and Hubs, most of the digital places are empty environments, as movie stage backdrops. Activities are still ongoing, and messages can be left behind for future travellers. However, it is quite common to encounter entire worlds with missing content due to broken links, and there are several instances where the login process fails, a situation that makes the world inaccessible.

Few platforms generally maintain this status for long, and in certain cases, it indicates that they are moving to the next stage, where the platform's worlds simply cease to exist.

FIGURE 5.5
Panoramic screenshot of Metatropolis in Active Worlds. Credit ActiveWorlds.com.

Digital Graveyard: The Time as Memory

A digital graveyard represents the final stage of abandoned worlds, or rather, the digital places that are no more. These spaces become inaccessible and are often preserved as non-interactive experiences. They stand as memories of what once were digital monuments to a once-thriving community. These worlds, now completely abandoned or shut down, leave few to remember their existence. They serve as a stark reminder of the ephemeral nature of digital spaces, regardless of their past significance. In some instances, even their main websites become inaccessible, and the only way to remember them is through the echoes found in the blogs and tutorials of those who were once users and creators of these worlds. Indeed, our own "30 Days in Active Worlds," as detailed in Chapter 1, is now lost in time; once a thriving world with a community and, in a short period of time, becoming one of the most popular spaces in the Metaverse, the world is now lost. The only reminder of the world is now this book, some previous academic papers and webpages archived by the Web Time Machine. The frontier was not preserved. It was turned off.

While writing this book, we observed the decline of two Metaverse platforms that ultimately became digital graveyards. The first was AltspaceVR, followed by Mozilla Hubs. AltspaceVR nearly vanished in 2017, but it was revived thanks to significant investment from Microsoft. Like other platforms, AltspaceVR used the concept of worlds and universes to group spaces together. Overall, the platform catered to a more mature audience compared to other VR social media available such as VRChat or REC Room. Microsoft also sought to capture the business market by offering a workplace-oriented version of AltspaceVR, named Microsoft Mesh and still available but substantially different form AltspaceVR. The platform was well-regarded in the education sector, hosting regular meetups by the group Educators in VR, and provided a communal space for interaction and community building, thanks also to the possibility of creating unlimited worlds for free.

Despite its usage, the absence of direct monetisation strategies and shifting interests from Microsoft led to the platform's closure. Users were informed of a specific shutdown date, March 10, 2023, at 1 pm Eastern Time, also in order to retrieve some of their data. The known date and time allowed some community members to gather one last time, witnessing the end of the AltspaceVR Metaverse platform together. This event, captured by several users, remains accessible online. It may be the first instance where the "end of the world," often portrayed in films and literature, was experienced and recorded within a digital platform. Indeed, it echoes, digitally, the Restaurant at the End of Universe by Douglas Adams. The voices are cut over, the avatars are frozen, and the worlds are not accessible anymore, with a final message from the team to thank the users (Figure 5.6).

In the months before AltspaceVR's closure, discussions shifted to identify alternative meeting spaces and potential worlds for relocation. Platforms like Spatial.io expressed readiness to welcome the displaced AltspaceVR community, inviting them to bring their content and assets.

As we have seen, the second platform that was planned to be discontinued was Mozilla Hubs. In this instance, the announcement was similar to that

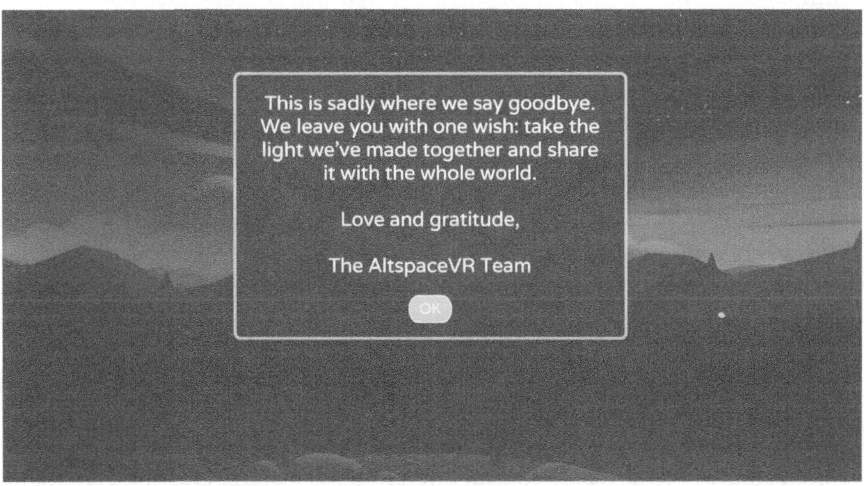

FIGURE 5.6
AltspaceVR were shut down on March 10, 2023, at 1 pm Eastern Time. The worlds after this time were not accessible anymore, and a message from the developer team was welcoming the users in the last moment of its existence. Credit Cause + Christi.

of AltspaceVR, made a few months before the planned shutdown on May 31, 2024, at 12 am PDT. However, there is a significant difference from the AltspaceVR case. The Mozilla Hubs community, anticipating the shutdown, has provided comprehensive documentation not only to retrieve the data of each room created and content uploaded but also detailed instructions to replicate the Mozilla Hubs infrastructure on private servers, utilising its open-source components. Although the central Hub servers are now decommissioned, the creation of private instances is still possible, ensuring the persistence of these worlds.

Reasons for Abandonment

The examples we provided across three categories—abandoned worlds, digital ruins, and digital graveyards—illustrate some of the reasons that cause the decay of digital landscapes from the perspectives of both the users and the technology involved. In the ever-shifting digital world, research on new trends can draw users away from one platform to another, which has risen in popularity.

Emerging platforms often offer unique experiences and features, or they present monetisation opportunities for content previously available for free. Over time, the initial excitement for a digital world may fade, often due to the novelty wearing off or the realisation that the digital environment has not fulfilled the expectations established at its launch. A Metaverse may become obsolete if it does not evolve with its users' needs or if new platforms better serve those needs. The survival of a digital platform is linked to its adaptability; those who succeed are the ones who pivot their content to match the shifting interests of their users. An example is Spatial.io, which introduced a series of gamified experiences in 2023, aligning with the gaming industry's direction and adding value to the Metaverse experience beyond the common gathering place. This pivot was in clear contrast to Spatial's earlier focus in 2020 on collaboration and productivity for organisations, branding itself as a space where one could "Collaborate from anywhere in AR." In 2024, the platform rebranded itself as a "3D gaming hub." Yet trends move quickly and at the time of writing, April 2025 with it now pivoting to the tagline—Interactive Media, Limitless Possibilities: Harness Spatial Computing and AI to unlock the next generation of interactive virtual worlds.

From the technical side of view, the end of these platforms often stems from a confluence of technological and strategic factors. Hosting servers for these environments has high costs, leading to shutdowns if a company struggles financially if the user base declines over time, or if the infrastructure owner decides to focus on other initiatives. This was the case with Mozilla Hubs, which was abandoned following a strategic pivot into other products unrelated to the Metaverse hype. Furthermore, the underlying technology might become outdated due to newer, more profitable standards, leaving the users unable to access the client software. Platform preferences also play a critical role. When a particular platform is favoured over another, it can result in the abandonment of the less popular Metaverse. This preference could be influenced by a variety of factors that ultimately determine the lifespan of the Metaverse's worlds.

Post-Abandon, the Museum of the Metaverse

The explorations conducted to date are far from conclusive, opening up further directions for research. Across both abandoned and nearly abandoned digital places, our initial exploration has revealed that the promises of the digital frontier's immutable and everlasting presence, which often capture our imagination, are, in fact, not true. The passage of time defines a similar influence on these virtual spaces as it does on the physical worlds they overlay, augment, or replace.

Looking at these places from the abandonment process can inform our understanding of the Metaverse's next phase. Considering the platform that we had the opportunity to explore it is evident that no single solution is universally applicable. Both decentralised and centralised strategies for developing and maintaining worlds, islands, and rooms have their merits and drawbacks, and they both could lead to the process of decay we described.

There is a clear contrast between highly customisable environments and their less adaptable counterparts, which contribute to maintaining activity in certain digital worlds as they significantly impact user perception and engagement. This has been observed in platforms like Second Life and Active Worlds. The ability to create and personalise a space likely fosters a sense of ownership and connection, thereby enhancing the user's investment in renovating and maintaining the content of the environment itself. However, a high level of customisation can also lead to an exponential expansion and multiplication of digital worlds, affecting their visibility and accessibility and potentially impacting the cost of infrastructure. More challenging to address is the motivations and demographics of users engaging with these worlds. These can vary widely, and the constant need for additional content and forms of engagement demands responsiveness from the platforms that may not always be possible to provide and fulfil.

While it seemed undeniable that major brands play a role in the rise or fall of Metaverse worlds, our exploration reveals that this is just one facet of a larger picture. Platforms driven by robust communities have demonstrated resilient collective strength. When technological limitations were the main obstacles to the continuity of these environments, in certain cases, and when allowed, community-led solutions, mimicking the original platforms, emerged to support the existence of these places.

Moreover, when user interest shifted, some platforms attempted to rebrand themselves to stay relevant to prevailing trends. This was evident in numerous cases that tried to reinvent the workplace during the pandemic lockdown, which fell short of replacing the physical workplace once restrictions were lifted and the "new normal" did not look significantly different from the "normal." Only a few managed to integrate successfully into existing processes and continue to exist. In this context, the emerging trend appears to be shifting towards an "augmented desk" rather than a virtual office. This is evident in the marketing pitches and applications supported by companies like Apple, Meta, and Niantic, where the multiplicity of the Metaverse blends with the physical environment itself. On the other hand, platforms that actively promote activities and regularly introduce updates, particularly those focused on gaming or events, tend to be the driving forces of the Metaverse, as demonstrated by their ability to attract a larger, more committed user base.

Observing the abandonment of the Metaverse's worlds and their decay into digital graveyards has led us to question: what purpose do these abandoned worlds serve? It is clear that the collective impact of these experiences has inspired and influenced subsequent platforms, establishing paradigms that, in certain cases, facilitated the affordance of the newer platforms. However, the same paradigms can also obstruct the growth of the Metaverse when the applied approaches maintain a too strong connection with the physical counterpart, limiting the exploration of novel forms of representation of spaces and times.

As we have seen in our explorations, content creation is an important aspect of the Metaverse, and the volume created across the vast number of platforms until now is staggering. Some content exists independently of the worlds from which it originated and can be reused and seen across multiple environments, while other content remains intrinsically linked to the confines of its original platform and, in certain cases, may eventually be lost forever.

In this context, the concept of museums in the Metaverse and the evolving role of digital collections play a pivotal role. Examples of such applications already exist, such as the Museo del Metaverso, which was established in 2009 with the purpose of archiving content from various Metaverse platforms. Initially launched in Second Life, these initiatives later transitioned to CraftWorlds and expanded to Spatial.io. The interest focuses on the content that was purposefully created for the Metaverse's world itself rather than being a transposition of physical collections into the digital environment as a form of preservation.

Thus, we wonder what form and function a museum dedicated to the lost worlds and digital graveyards would take. Such places and the creations they preserve could leave a lasting legacy for the future, prompting us to consider the role of intangible heritage created within the digital domain. The nature of preservation could range from maintaining the worlds in their abandoned state, where time is suspended as in a time capsule, to the opposite extreme, where the vibrancy of these spaces is preserved. In digital environments, such possibilities are not only conceivable but practically implementable. The use of non-player characters (NPCs) is already prevalent across most of these platforms, serving various roles, from providing information and guidance to onboarding users in the digital space. In gaming environments, NPCs help maintain a lively and engaging atmosphere, although their implementation has received mixed reactions from gamers due to their limited or overly skilled behaviours. However, the advent of artificial intelligence (AI) and large language model applications create opportunities to populate these environments. NPCs enhanced with conversational AI could not only fulfil existing needs but also potentially act as custodians and caretakers of these digital spaces. Whether this leads to a utopian or dystopian outcome remains to be seen, and ethical considerations regarding the original creativity that made these worlds memorable are vital and a reflection on the costs associated with keeping these spaces operational opens a dialogue on sustainable preservation in the long term.

What such a collection will look like remains an open field for exploration. We can catch a glimpse of this through Italo Calvino's description of Eutropia in "The Invisible Cities," which resonates as a fitting parallel to our discussions on abandoned worlds:

> *When he enters the territory of which Eutropia is the capital, the traveller sees not one city but many, of equal size and not unlike one another, scattered over a vast, rolling plateau. Eutropia is not one, but all these cities together; only one is inhabited at a time, the others are empty, and this process is carried out in rotation.*

The abandoned worlds and digital graveyards we have explored represent the forgotten corners of the Metaverse, remnants of past digital frontiers left behind as users gravitate towards newer experiences. While these lost realms may seem like mere relics, their existence prompts deeper questions about the preservation of our digital heritage and creativity. As we stand amidst the ruins of these virtual landscapes, one glimpse of the future for these worlds is a reopening and repopulation via AI.

The rapid advancement of AI technology, from conversational agents to generative models, opens up intriguing possibilities for populating and maintaining the digital environments once teeming with human activity. The abandoned worlds stand as a bridge between the Metaverse's past and its AI-driven future, challenging us to envision new frontiers where human ingenuity and AI converge in ways we have yet to imagine. We explore this further in the following chapter entitled "Turing's Dream."

6

Turing's Dream

Artificial intelligence (AI) has transitioned from science fiction to the practical tool that empowers us to automate tasks once thought impossible. It has become an everyday reality, transforming the way we live, work, and interact with one another. Those same technologies are blurring our perception of reality in the Metaverse and playing a crucial role in enabling the creation of realistic and immersive virtual environments.

Since its inception at the Dartmouth conference in 1956, artificial intelligence has progressed significantly as a research domain. The formulation of the Turing test, alongside the establishment of foundational concepts like symbolic reasoning and machine learning, has catalysed advancements across a spectrum of modern computing fields. AI's influence extends to diverse domains, ranging from natural language processing (NLP) and computer vision to robotics and machine learning. However, its potential impact goes far beyond these individual domains. In the next phase of technological evolution, AI will play a crucial role in shaping a Metaverse that looks and feels indistinguishable from the world around us. As we continue to explore and develop our digital landscape, AI will provide the tools for creating systems that feel more intelligent, with an ability to learn, adapt, and make decisions in real-time. AI will be a key technology enabling the full potential of the Metaverse, providing us the means to create new forms of communication, collaboration, and creativity that were previously unimaginable.

In this chapter, we introduce key elements of AI research that are already changing the way we build and interact with the Metaverse. These behind the scenes building blocks are often not directly visible but are influencing most of the action in the environment. One of the key concepts in AI relevant to the development of the Metaverse is machine learning (ML). ML is a subset of AI that enables computers to learn from data without being explicitly programmed. This simple concept has been transformative given the exponential growth of data afforded by the internet. In the past couple of decades, we have been collecting pictures, videos, stories, songs, and many other sources of data. In turn that has been tagged with descriptive information such as colour, subject, location, and indexed by search engines so that others can find it. This explosion of data is providing the raw materials from which we are using machine learning to generate our future Metaverse. For example, an ML algorithm could be trained on a dataset of images of forests and use this training to generate a photorealistic virtual forest in the Metaverse.

DOI: 10.1201/9781003440437-6

In the following sections we explore key AI technologies impacting the Metaverse. We discuss how NLP is being used to create more human-like interactions with NPCs, as touched upon in previously in Chapter 4. As well as increasing accessibility through making environments more inclusive and responsive to individual user abilities and preferences or through translation and localisation. We explore how AI is being used to power content creation through generative design tools, and introduce how machine vision enables computers to interpret and understand visual data from the real world. The section on enhancing realism introduces emerging techniques such as neural rendering, spatial audio and dynamic world simulation as examples of work towards creating lifelike experiences using cutting-edge advancements in AI and immersive technologies.

However, amidst the promise of these technological advancements, history shows us that it is essential to consider the ethical implications and potential challenges that AI presents. As we create these tools on our journey to build the Metaverse, we must navigate carefully, addressing concerns and ensuring that AI serves as a force for positive transformation while mitigating any unintended consequences that may arise. We conclude the chapter commenting on some of ethical challenges we will encounter and the socio-economic impacts of how these technologies will reshape industries, economies, and society at large.

To Be Human in a Virtual World

Have you recently been interacting with an online chat service and not been sure if you are speaking with a person or a robot? That question was at the heart of an idea proposed by Alan Turing to test if a computer could exhibit intelligence. In his 1950 paper titled "Computing Machinery and Intelligence," published in the journal *Mind*, he proposed a game where a person interacts with either another person or a computer program through text-based communication. In the game the player provides written questions and receives written answers from either the computer or the other person. The goal is for the person to determine whether they're talking to a human or a computer. This doesn't necessarily mean the answers are right or wrong, only that the computer can fool the person into thinking it's human. If it can, then it passes the Turing test. Whilst the test described above focuses on a text based input and output, its focus is on testing indistinguishability of the two competing actors in the game. This text version of the game can also be extended to other forms of nonverbal human activity such as robotics.

The Turing test is a simple yet profound way to measure how close we are to creating artificial intelligence that can think and communicate just like we do. It also fuelled considerable discourse amongst philosophers who for centuries have debated the ability of machines or automata to exhibit intelligence, or what it means for a machine to think. The success of a Turing test largely depends on how you define success. In terms of creating AI systems that can pass for humans in casual conversation through text inputs, we've made significant progress. Chatbots or conversational AI programs are now at a fidelity that they can fool people into believing they're talking to another human, at least for a short period of time. However, passing the Turing test in a robust and consistent manner across various contexts and conversations remains a significant challenge.

While AI has advanced in NLP and understanding, there are still limitations in areas such as understanding context, nuanced emotions, and maintaining coherent conversations over extended periods. Additionally, the text input is just one sensory cue working in isolation. When you add in a voice element, or facial expressions, or the movement of someone's hands as they are talking, the difficulty of maintaining the illusion of indistinguishability becomes significant. We could also introduce all the other facets of artificial intelligence, such as problem-solving, creativity, and ethical decision-making, that are equally important but not directly assessed by the Turing test and you probably start to understand the complexity of creating a General AI—an AI that can perform any intellectual task that a human being can. It makes you realise the remarkable capacity of humans, metaphorically speaking, as machines.

So what does the intersection of AI and the Metaverse look like? What does it mean to be human or artificial within a virtual realm? In parallel to the philosophical debate on what it means to think, the technology to support the ability to compute in ways that make machines indistinguishable have been developing exponentially. Moore's Law, which observed that the number of transistors on a microchip was doubling approximately every two years with an increase in compute power and decrease in cost per transistor, was significant in creating a compute environment where available resources have continually doubled over the last half century. Whilst we may now be seeing some plateauing of that rate of change based on the physical limitations of transistor miniaturisation, the connectivity of compute and data resources afforded by the internet plus algorithmic advances and access to specialised hardware accelerators appear to provide a continued supply of technological growth.

The proliferation of digital data generated by various sources, such as social media, sensors, and connected devices, has provided AI systems with large and diverse datasets to learn from. At the heart of all machine learning algorithms is the idea of machines identifying patterns in the data. The complex combinations of zeros and ones that are too complex for us to explain but are simple enough for a machine to build a mathematical relationship. It is the abundance of data that has enabled more accurate training of AI models and facilitated the development of AI applications in the Metaverse. The development of algorithms such as deep learning, reinforcement learning, and generative adversarial networks have enabled systems to achieve human-level performance in areas such as image recognition. Coupled with the development of specialised hardware accelerators, graphics processing units (GPUs), and tensor processing units (TPUs), which are optimised for matrix operations typically found in neural network computations, the tools for accelerating the uptake of AI workloads has further boosted the performance and efficiency of AI workloads driving it into consumer applications.

Whilst Moore's law may be plateauing, the tools for developing AI are still accelerating. The re-emergence of deep neural networks in the mid-2000s kick started a resurgence in AI research that still continues today. Observing the development of AI techniques in the present day is challenging, but if you look back at the progress over the past year the change starts to look radical. Like many innovations or new technology it starts to disappear once we take it for granted. The face detector on your digital camera, or more likely your phone, is no longer perceived as an amazing bit of AI, it is just a function to allow it to focus on the object that matters. These small bits of fractional AI, when combined, are the materials that create the allusion of a virtual world where the machines can be our companions.

AI-Powered Content Creation

Behind every piece of content on the internet and our computers is an algorithm describing its properties. An algorithm is simply the abstract set of rules or procedures applied to solving some problem or completing a task. It is the recipe of the steps required to reach an objective. They are a core concept in computer science, providing a theoretical foundation and the practical tools for solving computational problems.

The 1970s text based adventure game Colossal Cave Adventure is an early example of a rules based system to govern interactions between objects and players. Whilst Adventure did not use what we would currently call a formal rule-based system based on formal logic, it did rely on a series of rules and procedures, algorithms, to inform gameplay. The text-based interface had a finite number of instructions the player could use to activate these rules, for example, "go north" or "get lamp." At the time, this novel form of exploratory gameplay provided an emergent and re-playable game environment and sowed the seeds for modern exploration focused games like No Man's Sky. Whilst they are games from different eras, the methods used to define their non-linear gameplay are similar. The difference is in the level of complexity in the rules being written. In Adventure, the rules and relationships were all hand crafted by the programmer, Will Crowther, and hard coded into the programme. In No Man's Sky an algorithm, seeded with a random number based on one of the developers phone numbers, is used to generate the algorithm.

AI has radically transformed our ability to create novel environments in which we can immerse ourselves. The potential for AI as a programming tool to autonomously generate assets such as art work, dialogue and gameplay mechanics, has had a significant impact on how we can efficiently create larger more realistic worlds by automating many content creation tasks and allowing developers to focus on the overall gameplay experience. World building and procedural content generation are two related concepts that highlight the potential for the use of AI to generate virtual environments and content in video games, simulations, and other digital media. While they share similarities, there are also key differences between the two.

Automated world-building involves the algorithmic creation of large-scale environments such as planets, continents, cities, and landscapes, as well as the placement of objects, buildings, and natural features within these environments. The goal is to create cohesive and immersive virtual worlds that users can explore and interact with, typically in open-world games, virtual reality experiences, or simulations. Examples of automated world-building include generating entire planets and star systems in space exploration games like No Man's Sky or expansive landscapes in open-world games like Grand Theft Auto and creating whole cities such as San Fransokyo in the film Big Hero 6 using tools such as CityEngine.

At a similar, but smaller, scale, procedural content generation typically refers to the generation of individual content elements or assets within a virtual environment using algorithms. Examples of content elements from the world of games include textures, objects, characters, levels, and the generation of gameplay elements such as enemy placements and level layouts. The focus here is usually on creating dynamic content that adapts to player interactions and preferences, enhancing the overall gameplay experience. Examples of procedural content generation include generating random dungeons and loot in roguelike games such as Spelunky, the thousands of planets in the 1980s adventure game Elite or the procedural animation techniques used in Pixar films to model the movement of hair and fur. Whilst the generation of entire virtual worlds and the generation of individual assets within those worlds have obvious overlaps, both techniques play important roles in game development and digital media, offering ways to create immersive and engaging experiences for players and users.

Automated World-Building

From the vast and varied landscapes of Minecraft to the lush environment of the alien planet Pandora in the film Avatar, algorithms have been used to procedurally generate the virtual worlds around us. The techniques used to create these environments come from a variety of sources including mathematics, complexity theory and biology. In No Man's Sky, the generation of fauna and flora, terrain, weather, indeed the creation of whole planetary systems, showcases the variety of algorithms commonly used in world building.

Noise functions, such as Perlin noise and simplex noise, are mathematical algorithms used to generate random variations and patterns in procedural content. These functions generate pseudo-random variations in terrain height, surface details, and environmental features, resulting in realistic and visually natural-looking landscapes, textures, and visual effects. One of the most widely used and influential noise functions, Perlin noise, was originally developed in 1983 by Ken Perlin. Developed in response to his frustration with the machine-like computer generated images of the time in films like Tron, his goal was to develop an algorithm that would produce natural textures directly onto three dimensional objects. This allowed the algorithm to be applied to solid objects and as such had a very low overhead since the same mathematical function was used to carve out the texture from the virtual solid. This process meant that as Moores law scaled, the intricacy of the textures being carved also grew in complexity.

At the heart of this algorithmic approach are several parameters that can be adjusted to control the characteristics of the generated noise. For example, there are parameters to determine the appearance, scale, and complexity of the noise pattern. A frequency parameter controls the level of detail and complexity of the pattern. The higher the frequency the smaller the details and the finer the pattern. The amplitude parameter determines the overall magnitude or intensity with a higher value giving more emphasis to variations in high and low values and smaller values making things look smoother. Octaves refer to the number of layers of iterations that are built up to create a final noise pattern and lacunarity are the rate at which those successive octaves increase. These parameters, and others, can be adjusted to create a wide variety of noise patterns. This is also the opportunity for AI generated noise. Deep learning techniques can be used to fine tune these parameters to enhance the realism of the pattern in the noise. By training neural networks on large datasets of real-world textures, AI can learn to generate textures that closely resemble those found in the physical world by learning the relationships between input parameters and desired outputs. These models can be used to optimise the parameters of the Perlin noise based on desired texture characteristics such as roughness or smoothness. Or the model can introduce additional features to add finer detail or variations based on learned patterns. The models can also be used to transform textures to match specific visual styles or to create specific artistic effects. For example, the texture of a brick wall generated with Perlin noise could be transformed to resemble a different material, such as wood or metal, or an artificially generated terrain map could be transformed using NASA's Shuttle Radar Topography Mission (SRTM) elevation map imagery to generate geomorphically realistic worlds.

Related approaches to generating terrain models include the diamond-square algorithm, a procedural algorithm used to generate height-maps. Its name describes the process of taking the midpoint of each square grid in the scene and computing the midpoint elevation by averaging the value at each corner and adding a random displacement, which is decayed over time to determine the coarseness of the terrain. The procedure is then repeated for each of the diamonds created as a result of dividing up the squares. These two steps, square and diamond, are then repeated iteratively. The resulting height map appears smooth and flowing like real terrain, with the ability to control the average height and coarseness easily. This technique for automated world building creates realistic terrain features such as mountains, valleys, and plains. It is often used alongside the complimentary technique of Voronoi diagrams which use geometric structure to partition space into regions based on the distance to a set of points called seeds. In automated world building this technique is often used to distributed entities such as settlements or resources. For example, the terrain topology generated by the diamond-square algorithm can affect the suitability of different areas for settlement and the Voronoi diagrams can be used to create regions corresponding to settlement territories with each region encompassing a cluster of population centres. Similar to the Perlin noise approach, AI can be used to optimise parameter selection and realism of the terrain, plus learning to predict optimal resource distribution or simulation of population dynamics.

These techniques used to create complex and intricate terrain formations, such as coastlines, mountains, and valleys, simulate natural geological processes to generate realistic and varied landscapes. One of the super powers of these fractal geometries is that they exhibit self-similarity at different scales. They appear similar when viewed at different levels of magnification. Fractal algorithms can generate realistic cloud formations, water ripples, or geological formations such as canyons. Their properties allow for the creation of visually convincing and dynamically changing natural features within virtual environments.

Procedural Content Generation

Procedural content generation has many similarities to automated world building, but tends towards a different scale. It is used to automate the generation of content in digital environments such as games, simulations, or virtual worlds. In film the techniques are used by animators to generate complex and visually stunning effects without manually animating each element. In set design, virtual sets can be dynamically generated to suit different scenes, saving time and resources compared to traditional set construction. In generative music algorithms generate melodies, harmonies, and rhythms based on musical rules, random variations, or user input, creating dynamic and immersive musical experiences. In learning environments simulations provide realistic and immersive training environments where trainees can practice skills, scenarios, and decision-making in a safe and controlled manner. Similar to the techniques described for automated world building, at the core of the technology behind procedural content generation are the algorithms that use AI to help automate the process of diverse, dynamic, and immersive content creation.

No Man's Sky provides a case study for describing how AI is being used to enhance the realism and infinite feeling of the immersive world. By using procedural generation to create a universe of 18 quintillion planets it offers players a near-infinite exploration experience, with each planet being unique in terms of terrain, flora, fauna, and environmental conditions. Take for example the flora and fauna. L-systems, Lindenmayer systems, are used as part of the procedural generation process to generate the branching structures and patterns of plant life found on planets. These algorithms define rules for how plant structures grow and evolve, including parameters such as branching angles, segment lengths, leaf placement, and other characteristics. By using L-systems, No Man's Sky is able to create a wide variety of plant forms and structures, from towering trees to intricate shrubs and vines, with a high level of complexity and realism.

L-systems are a type of formal grammar that specify simple rules for growth and branching. The grammar describes the parameters used by the algorithm to enhance diversity, realism, and visual appeal of the generated vegetation. These parameters such as the axiom (initial shape of the plant), production rules (how the symbols are replaced in each iteration), angle parameters (the orientation of branches and foliage), branch length and thickness, etc., can all be optimised through techniques such as genetic algorithms, reinforcement learning, or neural networks. Examples of these branching structures and the code used to generate them are highlighted in Figure 6.1. Animals are created from the procedural distortion of archetypes, mixing and matching random parts from a library but then tuning based on an underlying skeleton to maintain realism of the creature. Their behaviours are coded through adding agent like rules describing the objects they have an affinity towards. These attributes drive behaviours such as seeking out objects they like and avoiding those they don't. These procedurally generated fauna and flora contribute to the richness and diversity of the game's planet ecosystems, enhancing the sense of immersion and exploration for players.

One of the key attributes of algorithms used to procedurally generate objects and worlds is the deterministic reproducibility of their algorithm. This means that a planet generated in an 18 quintillion planetary system will be the same for each player. More importantly it means it will be the same for you if you return at a later time. It is also a very efficient way to codify the information for distribution. There are many different algorithms and

FIGURE 6.1
2D L-systems trees. (Wilson 2025, https://github.com/djdunc/djdunc.github.io/blob/main/projects/Lsystems/L_systems.ipynb)

techniques that take a similar approach, each having subtle differences in the different types of content or contexts in which they can be used. For example, fractal algorithms are often used for terrain generation due to their ability to produce natural-looking landscapes with self-similar properties. Similarly, cellular automata that evolve over time based on the states of neighbouring cells may be used for generating patterns or simulating growth processes, while the stochastic nature of Markov chains that describe a sequence of events where the probability of each event depends only on the state of the previous event, can be employed for generating sequences or narratives. Procedural generation, in all its forms, is a key component of the Metaverse if we want to enable the creation of vast, diverse, and dynamic virtual worlds that adapt and evolve based on user interactions.

Avatar Creation and Customisation

One unique characteristic of every Metaverse is the human participation. The avatars that represent our presence serve as the primary means of how others see us in that world. They form our identity, they provide our means of social connection and they have the potential to enhance, or hinder, the collaborative nature of the Metaverse experience. In training and simulation, the importance of representing other human users can be key to supporting a level of immersion that feels real. Medical students can use avatars representing patients with different medical conditions or symptoms to practice conducting medical histories, performing physical examinations, and making diagnostic decisions. Allowing students to explore the human body in a virtual environment can help them understand the complexity of our anatomical structure and provides them with a platform for endless practice and repetition. This allows students to develop their clinical skills in a safe and controlled environment.

The appearance of your avatar can also impact your own performance. Psychologists suggests that in real life people learn better from trainers who are similar to themselves and studies in VR have shown similar results. It suggests that creating an avatar that reflects your perception of self in the most basic ways, gender, body shape, hair, and skin colour, can improve your effectiveness to learn new skills. The fidelity of the avatar also impacts the perceived reality of your immersive experience with a lifelike avatar benefiting from greater social presence and credibility. Social presence implies they seem more real and more able to convey emotions and intentions. In contexts where credibility is important, such as education where an avatar is meant to represent a real person or expert, users may require avatars to appear more lifelike to establish authority.

Whilst the idea of lifelike avatars sounds simple, it has proven incredibly difficult to implement. One of the biggest challenges has been the innate human ability to see something that is not quite right. The concept of the Bukimi no Tani (Uncanny Valley) was introduced by Japanese roboticist Masahiro Mori in 1970. His work explored the relationship between human likeness in robots and the emotional response elicited from observers. He hypothesised that as robots become more human-like, we become increasingly positive and empathetic towards them until a point at which the likeness becomes almost human which results in a strong negative emotional response. As the appearance continues to get more human-like the response returns to being a positive one, hence the reference to the uncanny valley. This concept is widely recognised in various fields such as robotics, animation, and artificial intelligence.

In the context of avatars, the uncanny valley is important when designing virtual characters or assistants. When an avatar looks too human-like but lacks certain human qualities such as realistic facial expressions or natural movements, it can evoke feelings of unease in users. Designers aim to navigate the uncanny valley by creating avatars that strike a balance between human likeness and stylisation, avoiding the creepy zone where slight imperfections become highly noticeable. Advances in AI and animation technology continue to push the boundaries of creating more lifelike avatars while minimising the uncanny valley effect.

Two key AI algorithms currently being used to develop AI avatars using deep learning are Variational Autoencoders (VAEs) and Generative Adversarial Networks (GANs). VAEs are used to learn the underlying structure of facial features so that they can then generate new faces that mimic human-like characteristics. Using a large dataset of facial images, the VAE is trained to compress the facial data into a lower-dimensional latent space, where it can capture the essential features and relationships between them. The AI system then generates new faces by sampling from the learned distribution in the latent space. By adjusting the parameters of the VAE, developers can control the level of realism, expression, and diversity in the generated avatars. GANs consist of two neural networks, a generator and a discriminator, trained in an adversarial manner. The generator is trained to produce synthetic faces that can deceive the discriminator, a network that classifies images as real or fake. As the training progresses, the generator learns to generate more realistic and diverse facial features, while the discriminator becomes better at detecting generated faces from real ones supplied in the training data. This adversarial process drives the improvement of both networks, allowing for the creation of highly realistic AI avatars that can mimic human-like expressions, emotions, and even movements.

As the demand for personalisation develops and the infrastructure supporting the Metaverse grows, the software tools for developing AI avatars that fuel that growth are now becoming commonplace. Examples include software such as StyleGAN, designed by NVIDIA and released ad open source in 2019 that allows the creation of photorealistic faces, MetaHuman by Epic Games, a framework for Unreal Engine to create and animate highly realistic digital human characters, and Synthesia, a platform that utilizes GANs and VAEs to generate realistic human avatars with diverse characteristics.

Broadening Modes of Interaction

At the start of this chapter we questioned whether you had ever been unsure if you were chatting to a bot or a human. The technology behind the ability for computers to communicate in a way that feels natural to us has made enormous progress since the early days of conversational AI systems such as the Stanford Research Institute developed Elisa. One of the key technologies at the heart of that system was NLP, the ability of computers to understand, interpret, and generate human language. The algorithms behind NLP are based on concepts such as: Tokenisation, breaking the text into individual tokens representing words; Part of Speech tagging, identifying the grammatical characteristics of the token (noun, verb, etc.); Dependency Parsing, looking at sentence structure and the relationships between token (e.g., subject—verb—object); Sentiment Analysis, using ML to classify the emotional tone of the text (e.g., positive, negative, neutral). Whilst Elisa did utilise concepts which we would recognise today as NLP it also relied heavily on a rules-based system to support the process of responding to natural language queries since it was operating under very different technological constraints and capabilities.

Today, Large Language Model (LLM) technologies are ingesting a vast corpus of written text with billions of words. In the race to create the best model, the complexity of the neural network architectures and the scale of the computing infrastructure required to train and run inferences on the models continues to grow. In 2023, OpenAI's GPT-4 with an estimated 1.7 trillion parameters, was acknowledged as best of breed, with Anthropic, Mistral, Meta, and Google all working to catch up. However the differences between their performance has narrowed, as they are typically being trained on the same publicly available data, with some models producing similar or better scores on benchmark tests. This brings us to the old adage, a model is only as good as the data on which it is trained. Whilst LLM's are producing amazing results in terms of general conversational interfaces, that is also their limitation. These general purpose robots talk like humans that are not experts, but generalists. NLP may also suffer from the uncanny valley phenomena, for example, as a teacher it is quite easy to spot a report that has been written using an LLM, the language often does not align with the human author and words or phrases can feel incongruous.

In the Metaverse, NLP is playing an increasingly important role in enabling communication between humans and virtual entities. Voice-controlled interfaces are allowing users to interact with virtual characters and objects using natural language commands. In the same way that we may use Siri or Alexa to turn on BBC Radio 6 in our real world kitchen, these assistants can help humans navigate virtual spaces, provide guidance or answer questions, or perform tasks based on user requests such as asking for assistance with controlling a virtual object. These speech to text translations enable voice-based processing and interpretation of spoken language inputs, enabling seamless integration of voice interactions enhancing immersion and accessibility. This type of language-based user interface provides users with intuitive ways to engage with the Metaverse using natural language. Whilst general purpose AI chatbots in the Metaverse are still emergent, we are heading towards having our own versions of J.A.R.V.I.S. (Just a Rather Very Intelligent System), the AI that functions as Tony Stark's assistant in the film "Iron Man."

The use of dialogue in games with NPC's is an example of where NLP is starting to be used as a technology to create more realistic interactions in game play. Many games such as Skyrim, Fallout 4, Red Dead Redemption 2 all use conversational interfaces to create dialogue between player and NPC. Whilst these examples are probably using NLP like technologies to create the illusion of natural language interactions they hint at the direction of travel for these games. Combined with more realistic visual avatars the potential for more immersive and engaging interactions is enormous. When you also add into the mix gesture recognition that allows users to control their avatars movements by tracking body, hand, and facial movements, a more natural human like layer of expression can be added to their digital self.

Those immersive qualities will also change our personal interfaces with the Metaverse. In the world of chatbots our interactions are moving from bots that help us book tables at restaurants to more creative, personal, life-like AI companions. Inspired by fictional narratives such as those presented in the film *Her* and the dystopian *Black Mirror* episode *Be Right Back*, we are witnessing the emergence of chatbots such as Replika. These systems create a discursive environment for open ended conversation which in turn can support surface level companionship. While outliers often grab the headlines, for instance, the man who claimed his relationship with Replika saved his real-world marriage by inspiring him to reconnect with his wife, research shows that these chatbots can positively impact mental health and help manage feelings of depression and loneliness. Many of today's interactions with chatbots are still mediated through a text based input, but with services such as Replika we are starting to see the interfaces to these platforms merge into virtual reality.

Enhancing Realism

AI is helping us bridge the uncanny valley to create environments that don't cause us distraction. It is the combination of these many building blocks that are helping create the illusion of our mirror worlds and often those that are most supportive are the ones that are part of the background. They are the technologies that we don't necessarily perceive directly but have a significant impact on what we are experiencing. Examples include photorealistic rendering, spatial audio and dynamic world simulation.

In photorealistic rendering the goal is to make a 3D scene detailed and responsive to other elements in the virtual space that mimics how we perceive the real world. Neural rendering is a key AI technique being used to support the enhancement of visual fidelity. It uses deep neural networks for image or video generation that enable explicit or implicit control of scene properties. The process has three key components: the first is using generative neural networks to synthesise raw pixel information; the second is making the output controllable by interpretable parameters; and third making the scene properties such as illumination, geometry, or appearance controllable. One popular example in this pipeline is the use of Neural Radiance Fields (NeRF), a specific neural network based technique used to generate 3D scenes from 2D images by modelling the way light interacts with objects in the images. Rather than learning 3D voxel information, which can have large data storage requirements, the NeRF approach uses neural networks as a volume representation allowing for novel views of the scene to be rendered via ray-tracing—that is, they use an algorithm to output colour and opacity at a given x, y, z location.

An example that is starting to bridge our everyday real-world experience with those of our emerging use of the Metaverse is the humble use of maps to find out where we are going. Google's Block-NeRF has been used to develop city scale NeRF's based on collections of smaller NeRFs that can be rendered together to create a seamless transition. This stitching uses AI techniques called appearance embedding where a learned vector representation that captures the overall appearance of the individual scene is used so that alignment between two adjacent scenes can be optimised for rotation and translation. The benefit of dividing the scene into blocks is twofold, it not only decouples rendering time from scene size, it is also robust to changes over time as the appearance embeddings can adjust for things like time of day and exposure settings. As the fidelity of maps evolve from the symbolic representations of place to photo realistic mappings we can explore ex situ, this emerging digital twin of reality has the potential beyond the killer apps of tourism and real estate to enter into our mundane experiences of preparing for the day ahead. For example, checking if there is somewhere to park a motorbike outside a building, checking out if there is somewhere you can wait if you arrive early or doing a walk-through of the route from station to meeting place to check out if one route feels safer than another.

At the object level, tool makers are empowering creators to quickly and easily populate the Metaverse with diverse and realistic assets. NVIDIA's Instant NeRF enables the generation of detailed 3D environments and objects from simple 2D images. Meanwhile, tools such as Luma AI empowers users to capture real-world objects and people in 3D using their smartphones. Both these tools allow for the export of models into popular 3D software like Blender, for example the BlenderNeRF add-on, providing creators with the flexibility to further customise and refine their asset. The real world detail of these 3D models when integrated into virtual environments can enhance the realism of digital products and the personalisation of avatars discussed previously.

Combined with AI-driven audio technologies, what we hear in the Metaverse creates an increasingly immersive soundscape. Tools such as CassetteAI, with its advanced text-to-music capabilities, are being used by creators to generate dynamic music and sound effects that match the mood and atmosphere of a virtual environment. Utilising Latent Diffusion models, a type of generative model found in tools such as the popular text-to-image generator Stable Diffusion, they can also be used for text-to-audio generation. They use a similar technique of learning to remove noise from a signal that has been artificially added in the prior step, but in the case of audio this tends to be waveforms or spectrograms rather than images. The model is trained on pairs of noisy and less noisy audio representations, learning to predict the denoising steps. New audio is then generated by starting with random noise and iteratively applying the learned denoising models. Meanwhile, Dolby Atmos leverages object-based audio and AI algorithms to deliver precise spatial audio, placing sounds accurately in 3D space. This creates a sense of depth and realism. The combination of these technologies allows for the creation of multi-layered soundscapes that react dynamically to user interactions and environmental changes, further enhancing the feeling of presence and realism in the Metaverse.

Beyond just audio, AI is also being used to simulate complex ecosystems, weather patterns, and even the laws of physics, resulting in virtual worlds that evolve and react realistically to user interactions. The combination of these technologies allows for the creation of multi-layered soundscapes that react dynamically to user interactions and environmental changes, further enhancing the feeling of presence and realism in the Metaverse. AI-generated natural sounds, such as the gentle patter of rainfall or the rustling of leaves in the wind, deepen immersion by simulating real-world auditory cues, making the virtual world feel more tangible and alive.

By blending AI-powered audio and visual technologies, the Metaverse is rapidly evolving into a space that feels remarkably close to reality. Just as Google Maps' Immersive View fuses billions of images to create a rich, digital model of the world, AI-generated audio and spatial audio technologies are weaving an auditory tapestry that enhances the sensory experience within virtual environments. This convergence of technologies not only makes the Metaverse more engaging and enjoyable but also opens up new possibilities for communication, collaboration, and creative expression.

Improving Accessibility and Ethics

The Metaverse has the potential for significantly increasing inclusion through AI-driven interfaces that dynamically adapt to individual users. Intelligent systems that analyse user behaviour, preferences, and can adapt to varied abilities provide the opportunity for mass personalisation. For example, companies like Microsoft, in their work exploring hybrid work places, are developing AI-powered avatars that can interpret and respond to nonverbal cues, such as facial expressions and body language, making communication more accessible for users with speech or hearing impairments. Their Microsoft Mesh project, whilst not strictly in the Metaverse just yet, hints at the opportunities for making hybrid work in the Metaverse more accessible. AI-powered text-to-speech or image-to-text technology can convert written text into spoken words, allowing visually impaired users to access textual information. AI algorithms can automatically adjust the contrast and brightness levels of visual elements to make them more distinguishable for users with low vision. Or for the benefit of persons with low hearing, captions in

360° video that follow the viewer's gaze and indicate where sound is coming from. These approaches, if implemented to ISO standards, could ensure the Metaverse is not a one-size-fits-all environment but a dynamic space that caters to the diverse needs of its users.

The Metaverse has the potential to be borderless, and is already a melting pot of cultures and languages. AI-powered translation and localisation services are instrumental in breaking down language barriers, enabling seamless communication and collaboration between users from different regions. Whilst the Babel fish universal translator from Douglas Adams' fictional "The Hitchhiker's Guide to the Galaxy" might not be able to translate our thoughts yet, we are getting close to real-time translation. Platforms like Wordly.ai and Interprefy utilise AI to provide real-time translation of text and speech within virtual meetings and events. Additionally, AI algorithms can automatically translate in-world text, such as signs and menus, ensuring that users can navigate and interact with the environment regardless of their language. Localisation of content enhances the user experience and sense of belonging fostering a more connected and inclusive global community.

However, the Metaverse's reliance on AI-driven personalisation and interaction raises significant concerns regarding data privacy and security. As users engage with AI-powered avatars, translation services, and adaptive interfaces, vast amounts of personal data are collected, including biometric information, preferences, and behavioural patterns. This data trove becomes a prime target for potential misuse, from targeted advertising to identity theft. For instance, Meta (formerly Facebook) has faced scrutiny for its data collection practices within its social VR platforms, raising questions about how this data is used and protected. In 2024 the eight European Consumer Organisations (part of the BEUC network) launched a complaint against Meta around their extensive collection of user data, which included biometric data from VR platforms, stating that they were not adhering to GDPR.

The foundations on which the AI algorithms being integrated into the Metaverse also bring risks of perpetuating or amplifying existing biases. Whilst the launch of LLM's was largely seen as a positive technological advance there were also voices of concern over the transparency of the model. At the time of launch, OpenAI's GPT-3 language model was based on unfiltered content from the internet which also contained sexist and racist language. As a result the language used in response to prompts could become racist, sexist, and otherwise discriminatory. Prompts asking for descriptions of a good doctor often result in responses favoured to male characteristics. These biases, whether gender, racial, religious or other forms, can manifest in various ways, from discriminatory content recommendations to biased interactions with AI-powered characters. OpenAI, and other developers of LLM's, acknowledge these issues and actively work on mitigating biases in their models through various techniques, such as improved data filtering, bias detection tools, and fine-tuning with more diverse datasets. However, as language models get larger year on year, and the data used by the algorithms to spot patterns in the data increase, it feels like a Sisyphean task.

This rapidly evolving landscape of the Metaverse, however, does necessitate robust regulatory frameworks to ensure ethical AI use and to protect user rights. The European Union's proposed AI Act aims to address these concerns by establishing risk-based regulations for different AI applications. For example, in terms of transparency, generative AI would have to comply with EU Copyright law disclosing that the content was generated by AI. The collection and use of personal data, the potential for algorithmic bias, and the impact of AI on user behaviour all require careful consideration and regulation.

Artificial Intelligence is a key building block of the Metaverse, transforming it into an immersive environment that blurs the lines between the physical and digital worlds. AI-powered content creation, NLP, and machine vision are converging to create a more human-centric experience where users can interact with realistic virtual characters and environments in intuitive ways. Through advancements in neural rendering, spatial audio, and dynamic world simulation, AI is enhancing realism, making the Metaverse feel more lifelike and engaging. AI is breaking down barriers to entry by increasing accessibility, enabling individuals with diverse abilities and preferences to fully participate in this digital frontier. As we harness AI's transformative power, we must prioritise ethical considerations and address potential challenges to ensure that the Metaverse evolves into a space that is not only technologically advanced but also inclusive, equitable, and reflective of our shared humanity. AI is not just a supporting player in the Metaverse, but a critical technology driving its evolution towards a more immersive and inclusive future.

7

Digital Habitation and Future Worlds

Prediction is very difficult, especially if it's about the future.

Nils Bohr, Nobel laureate in Physics

We find ourselves on the precipice of a digital revolution, an inhabited Metaverse comprised of a blend of human-controlled and machine-controlled avatars. This is arguably the third wave of hype around the Metaverse, yet it differs from its predecessors in that it is driven by the transformative power of artificial intelligence (AI). Cities have historically served as epicentres of change, progress, and invention, acting as crucibles in which the future is crafted. In the research laboratories of universities, the nascent start-up companies on the outskirts of town, and the technology corporations that have attained sufficient size to possess their own campuses, the future Metaverse is meticulously being planned and shaped.

Visions of future cities have often been characterised as an amalgamation of utopian and dystopian elements. From the sprawling, neon-illuminated cityscapes depicted in the film "Blade Runner" to the digitally rendered Metaverse of "Ready Player One," these worlds have transcended their roles as mere fictional constructs. They have served as mirrors reflecting societal aspirations and anxieties pertaining to our urban future. Our future is without question—digital—with space mirrored in the virtual realm of computers and populated by avatars. Cities will have their own digital counterparts, existing in a realm unconstrained by traditional geographical and physical limitations. Yet this is still a while off, such a future takes time to build.

State of the Metaverse

Presently, the Metaverse is in a developmental phase. Despite its considerable potential and perceived role as the future of human existence, the Metaverse is still in its early stages of development. The second wave of hype surrounding the Metaverse was sparked by Facebook, one of the world's

DOI: 10.1201/9781003440437-7

largest corporations, fully embracing the concept and undergoing a name change to Meta. Apple has ventured into the realm of Spatial Computing with its Vision Pro, while Meta has introduced a new range of consumer-level devices through its Meta Quest 3 and has opened up its ecosystem for third parties to build headsets. Technological advancements have resulted in improved devices with sharper displays, a wider field of view, and faster processors enabling larger and more graphically rich environments. At the same time, network speeds have increased, facilitating the streaming of worlds from cloud-based services.

These digital devices merely represent the initial stage. The digital view is gradually being presented not as a floating image several inches in front of our eyes, as is the case with virtual reality (VR), or on the high dynamic range (HDR) enabled screens of contemporary laptops, but rather by directly beaming onto our retinas. Back in 2013, a headset called "Glyph" offered a glimpse into this potential future, eliminating the need for screens entirely. Instead, it employed a combination of optics to project an image directly onto the retina, effectively leveraging the back of the eyeball as a screen. Arguably ahead of its time, the resulting screen had a limited field of view, resembling the experience of sitting at the back of a cinema with a small screen. Nevertheless, it foreshadows the future and invites us to reconsider the current use of screens as a means of accessing the Metaverse, with the future beamed directly onto our retinas for a fully immersive experience. Combining this with standard glasses would enable a true augmented reality and facilitate data interchange between the Metaverse and the real world. It promises an era where digital information is not confined to screens but is seamlessly integrated with our physical surroundings.

In the current technological landscape, the Metaverse encompasses a wide range of devices and genres, including VR headsets, general computers, gaming consoles, and mobile devices. Within this spectrum, there are numerous Metaverses, with new ones emerging and others closing on a regular basis. It's a complex and evolving environment.

Yet amidst this complexity, the glimpses of the future that were so radiant in the late 1990s still persist, albeit in different manifestations. Active Worlds, once a pioneering platform, has sadly become mainly a ghost town with its software failing to catch up with modern standards. Second Life endures although it is also a shadow of what it was, while systems like Decentraland emulate its past success. Oncyber.io represents a vibrant alternative space, and Meta's Horizon has experienced a challenging start compared to other Metaverse systems, prompting discussions about how a prominent company like Facebook could have made such missteps. However, Meta's hardware and the ecosystem surrounding the Meta Quest headsets remain among the most competitive, cost-effective, and widely accessible in the market. They are arguably the future entry points into the Metaverse.

Within the realm of technological advancements and trends, diverse perspectives regarding the trajectory of the Metaverse have emerged.

Some hold the opinion that it is experiencing a decline, citing diminishing numbers and a potential retreat from its frontiers. However, evidence suggests otherwise, as substantial investments, emerging systems, and upcoming headsets, coupled with the involvement of key players like Meta and Apple, indicate a vibrant and evolving landscape. Despite Apple's circumspect approach in using the term "Metaverse" in its marketing materials, the potential for a Metaverse experience on its headsets remains palpable. As their vision continues to evolve, the future of the Metaverse will likely shift from questioning its viability to exploring its myriad potential directions. Central to this evolution is the representation of individuals in the Metaverse through avatars, heralding a future where we increasingly log into the Metaverse, traversing the boundary between our physical and digital existences. This phenomenon, which we term "Digital Habitation," signifies an increasing proportion of our lives being spent in the Metaverse, mediated through our avatars.

Avatars

The evolution of avatars has been remarkable, progressing from the limited capabilities of Active Worlds avatars, which were merely able to wave or dance, to Horizon's advanced facial tracking technology. Meta's Horizon now allows for the tracking of facial features, including lips, blinking, eyebrows, and eye direction. Sony has introduced full-body movement capability through additional wearables, and advancements in AI have made it possible to create photorealistic digital twins of individuals within the Metaverse.

However, the challenge of translating real-life movements into the virtual realm has remained unsolved until recently. Sony's motion-tracking technology addresses this issue, but it raises questions about potential collisions in physical spaces while wearing a headset and engaging in virtual activities. Current solutions for avatar movement primarily involve teleportation or flying, which do not accurately convey the experience of walking in a digital environment (Figure 7.1).

The start-up organisation "Omni One" aims to confront this obstacle through the introduction of the Omni One, a pioneering home-based solution that facilitates comprehensive bodily motion, encompassing walking, running, crouching, and jumping while adorned with a VR headset. The Omni One is characterised by a rotating foundation akin to a treadmill, albeit providing a 360-degree range of movement. A pivoted harness situated around the waist region impedes individuals from running off the system, consequently enabling unconstrained ambulation, running, and jumping within the prescribed boundaries of the unit. This innovation constitutes a significant stride towards resolving the challenge of locomotion within the

FIGURE 7.1
The Omni One. Credit Virtuix—https://virtuix.com/.

Metaverse and bears resemblance to the trackpad featured in the cinematic production "Ready Player One."

Going forward, avatars will build upon existing technological advancements, evolving into increasingly realistic and lifelike representations with attributes becoming indistinguishable from those of actual human beings. While the contemporary trend of customising avatars might result in short-lived popularity, there is a possibility that future iterations of avatars could be visually indistinguishable from our physical selves, featuring clothing, hairstyles, and overall appearances that dynamically adapt. All of these will be added to our avatars via the purchasing of digital assets using digital currencies. The overlap between the real and digital will continue to grow to such an extent that when we purchase physical goods, such as shoes, clothes, and glasses, they are likely to come with digital versions wearable in the Metaverse.

Moreover, avatars will likely acquire the capacity to convey a broader spectrum of emotions. The inclusion of more intricate emotions and nuances of non-verbal communication will augment online interactions and bolster the sense of immersion in the Metaverse. The ability to engage in tactile interaction not only through the hands but also with broader regions of the body is also imminent, resulting in further deepened levels of interaction and immersion. Such advancements demand prudent implementation but are anticipated to become a reality within the Metaverse system in the ensuing years. Combining these factors with the ability to replicate bodily movements and walk freely will enable avatars to represent individuals across a far more comprehensive range of activities than is presently possible in the Metaverse. This has the potential to revolutionise activities within the Metaverse, allowing individuals to be fully present in an alternate realm, all from the comfort of their own dwellings.

Consequently, the entire concept of homes may undergo a paradigm shift; when the Omni One walking system encompasses the entire floor and sensory inputs ranging from touch to smell are integrated into the Metaverse, our digital habitations may become our primary places of residence. With the physical world relegated to a space primarily for sleeping and sustenance, individuals may increasingly transition into their digital dwellings. Even when you are back in your physical world, your avatar may continue occupying the digital space via AI, essentially waiting for your return.

All of this so far is in the near future. Extending further, there is the prospect of Neurotechnology. This field aims to develop implantable brain-computer interfaces (BCIs) for treating neurological disorders and eventually merging human brains with AI. Currently, work on developing these devices is ongoing, with early testing of a Neuralink device (a company founded by Elon Musk in 2016) allowing a patient to play chess on a screen by merely thinking of the moves. The potential of Neurotechnology is substantial, ranging from addressing neurological disorders to enabling humans to interface with AI directly. Neurotechnology has the potential to allow direct control of avatars in the Metaverse using thought alone. This would offer a level of immersion far surpassing traditional controllers, keyboards, or even gesture-based systems. It would provide sensory feedback, allowing users to feel virtual environments or even the touch of an avatar, with tactile sensations fed directly into our nervous systems. This would be combined with the ability for users to share experiences or specific sensory perceptions with others in real-time, creating a new layer of social interaction within the Metaverse. If we link the ability to perform actions such as walking, running, jumping, and crouching and have these movements reflected digitally, in conjunction with senses of touch, eye tracking, and broader control via implants, we may reach a point where we genuinely occupy the Metaverse. This opens a new chapter in our human existence where we are physically located in the real world but arguably living in the digital realm—true digital habitation with the Metaverse plugged directly into our brains.

Artificial Intelligence

Within the digital landscape, AI is anticipated to serve as the driving force behind the Metaverse, encompassing nearly every aspect of this virtual environment. Its rapid growth and ubiquitous integration will transform the current digital realm into the predicted metascapes. As previously mentioned, avatars in the Metaverse will embody a post-human existence, capable of navigating and replicating the movements of physical bodies. AI-driven avatars will revolutionise the concept of bots, far surpassing the capabilities of early bots like those found in Active Worlds. These AI-driven avatars, particularly when linked with advancements such as ChatGPT, will transform into all-knowing personal assistants. These AI entities will be pivotal in guiding users through the Metaverse, providing information, facilitating social interactions, and personalising experiences based on individual preferences. They will possess not only access to the vast knowledge available on the internet but also the ability to interact with and modify the virtual worlds.

With AI, world-building shifts from a primarily manual process to a more automated approach. Currently, constructing virtual environments involves meticulously placing blocks and windows one by one. However, the future is one where AI generates landscapes, characters, narratives, and scenarios on the fly, resulting in ever-changing and dynamic worlds. AI will be responsible for creating the future cities within the Metaverse, a feat that could be achieved instantaneously in contrast to the physical world. Rome could be built not in a day but in an instance. This advancement will contribute to a more expansive and dynamic Metaverse, although it may also lead to the expanse of vast, unpopulated areas.

Additionally, AI has the potential to enhance the interoperability of the Metaverse. As multiple Metaverse platforms continue to emerge, AI can be employed to ensure compatibility between these platforms, enabling the translation of data, avatars, and assets for seamless use across different virtual environments. AI will touch all aspects of our lives, with AI bots almost "living" in the Metaverse, taking a physical form but exclusively existing and interacting within the realms of the Metaverse.

Economics

Within the current economic landscape, the value of separate sections of the Metaverse is already comparable to that of a nation-state. Moreover, when considering the cumulative effect of multiple systems, it represents a significant portion of the global digital economy. Yet despite its substantial influence, it has remained largely concealed, receiving only minimal coverage in mainstream media, primarily in specialised financial publications. This indicates that despite its size, it is still in its initial stages of development and far from the mainstream.

Given its inherent complexity and interconnectedness with global economic systems, predicting the economic future of the Metaverse is arduous. One possible trajectory is an increasing integration of individuals into the Metaverse workforce. Roles such as developers, who work behind the scenes to craft the intricate systems that underpin virtual worlds, are among the obvious candidates. Furthermore, emerging markets such as digital architects and builders will witness a surge in demand. Just as a non-architect would find it challenging to design a physical structure in the real world, so too would they in the Metaverse. While construction may be expedited in the Metaverse, it still necessitates a specialised skill set that digital builders possess. Architects have been actively involved in the Metaverse since its inception in platforms such as Second Life. In fact, there have been instances of architects transitioning from real-world practice to focus solely on Metaverse design. While the same may not be entirely applicable to the role of builders as their skill set differs, there is undoubtedly a demand for individuals adept in Metaverse construction. This demand extends beyond the realm of AI and large-scale modifications, encompassing intricate details such as houses, real estate, retail outlets, and headquarters of major organisations, all of which require human-level attention to detail.

A similar dynamic is observed for content designers and creators. These specialised skills will be highly sought after, prompting individuals to include them on their resumes and professional profiles. As new systems emerge, a significant influx of individuals will be vying for virtual real estate, particularly in prime locations. This phenomenon mirrors the dot-com boom, where corporations aggressively acquired domain names. In the Metaverse, this trend repeats itself with the launch of each new system. Furthermore, markets within the Metaverse will exhibit greater volatility compared to the real world. The Metaverse altcoin market will witness cycles of booms and busts, characterised by the formation and subsequent bursting of speculative bubbles, only to be replaced by the next cycle. If one thing is for sure in predicting the future, it is that change is inevitable.

One of the enduring aspects of the Metaverse's economy will be its frontier nature, with new trends and innovations causing economic shifts, some of which may have repercussions in the physical world. However, as the Metaverse evolves and matures, it will likely encounter regulation and security measures enforced by established national and international financial institutions. Regulatory frameworks may include taxation and the requirement to declare the sale of digital assets in tax returns. Additionally, governments may seek a certain degree of economic interoperability, ensuring that assets from one virtual world retain their value and can be utilised in others. At the moment, it truly is the Wild West, and this is likely to be tamed. The frontier will become more established and stable.

This stabilisation may be facilitated through the creation of standards for the Metaverse. An open and inclusive Metaverse will necessitate the adoption of interoperability standards, work on which is already underway. Developed by the Metaverse Standards Forum (MSF), founded in June 2022, the MSF aims to foster the development and deployment of interoperability standards for an open and inclusive Metaverse through pragmatic action-based projects. The MSF boasts over 1,800 industry members, including major players in the technology sector.

While standards are undoubtedly beneficial, it is worth considering the possibility that the true Metaverse may emerge organically, with large systems evolving first and standards forming around them rather than vice versa. Enforced standards, while well-intentioned, have the potential to stifle the very innovation they seek to promote. Neal Stephenson, who coined the term "Metaverse" in his 1992 novel "Snow Crash," expressed scepticism regarding top-down prescriptive approaches to shaping the Metaverse. He advocated for a bottom-up approach, with as few absolute rules as possible, emphasising the need for builders to make their own decisions. Standards are, of course, beyond economics. They cover the entire system, from the rendering to the format of the 3D assets, through the background processes required to process economic transactions. Ultimately, there will be interoperability in the currencies of the Metaverse, possibly traded into sub-currencies, either national or according to new and emerging worlds. However it shapes up, it will be a simple way to buy, sell, and earn money in the Metaverse.

Cities of Tomorrow

There will be an increasing convergence of our physical and virtual realities where technology will permeate every facet of our lives. This technological integration will serve as a connective tissue between interactions and experiences, presenting both awe-inspiring possibilities and, more worryingly, a world full of advertising slogans. It is also happening fast, Metas Rayban Glasses are expected to have an Augmented Capacity in the near future and with it information about the city will be available in front of our eyes (Figure 7.2).

This overlay of digital information will extend across the city, from its landmarks to its cafes and bars, its shops, services, and ultimately also onto its population. Every asset of the city will have a digital overlay, an overlay which is only visible if you are wearing a digital device. This shift may also suggest a reduced reliance on our mobile phones is incoming. These devices will ultimately replace the current display technologies.

FIGURE 7.2
An augmented reality view of the city, Credit Authors.

Future Living

The outlook of augmented reality in eyewear presents a significant contrast to the concept of the Metaverse. Upon entering the Metaverse, the cleanliness and the absence of litter are immediately noticeable. The constant sunshine and perfect lighting reflect off the immaculate surfaces. However, upon exiting the Metaverse and returning to reality, a moment of adjustment is necessary to adapt to the clutter of reality, the various objects that require tidying, or the walls that might need repainting. While this may be more reflective of personal living conditions, even the most pristine homes or flats struggle to compare to the picturesque views and impeccable nature of the Metaverse. The latest Virtual and Augmented Reality Headsets (from both Apple and Meta) enable users to extend their living spaces almost magically by opening up a wall into a new dimension. These headsets have automatic room scanning capabilities, allowing them to identify and utilise surfaces for projecting information. In reality, views from actual windows in real life may not be ideal, overlooking a main road or a car park. However, in this extended reality, the view can be a live stream from a renowned location such as Times Square, a picturesque ocean vista, or any desired scene from the Metaverse. Cruise ships have already implemented a limited version of this concept by utilising screens in internal cabins that lack ocean views. These virtual windows provide a live stream of the ocean, offering a continuous visual experience.

Consequently, our homes in the future are expected to undergo a transformation. Urban living will become increasingly dense, accommodating more people per square metre within cities. Windows may become virtual, and our living spaces, while physically small, will become virtually limitless when connected to the Metaverse.

Cities serve as cultural and creative hubs, centres of commerce, service providers, and transportation nodes. In a future Metaverse world, even if virtual spaces mirror physical cities, the necessity for physical transportation to meetings, retail outlets, and entertainment venues such as cinemas may diminish. Arguably, we are already seeing this trend with Zoom and Teams meetings reducing the number of hours spent in the office, and entertainment switching towards streaming services accessible anywhere. Similar arguments have been made regarding online shopping. Despite these technological advancements, physical locations have largely retained their vitality. Humans inherently desire to interact with tangible objects, make eye contact, and engage in physical touch. In this regard, online shopping, streaming, and remote meetings have undoubtedly transformed work practices but have arguably yet had limited impact on the overall vibrancy of cities. The real impact may come when technology is able to replicate touch and the human experience of co-presence. Once that boundary is crossed, then space, place, and geography will be a diminishing return compared to logging into a virtual world.

Of course cities are constantly shifting, being replanned or responding to current trends, economic, social or political. One contemporary concept is that of the "15-Minute City" offering a compelling counterpoint to the vast metascapes of the digital realm. Coined by urbanist Carlos Moreno in 2021, the 15-Minute City advocates for a model where all essential services and amenities—work, education, healthcare, recreation—are accessible within a 15-minute walk or bike ride from one's home. This vision promotes the decentralisation of urban centers, fostering small hubs that prioritize human-scale living and sustainability. As the Metaverse promises a boundless digital experience, physical cities could simultaneously evolve towards more localised, self-sufficient units that encourage community interaction and reduced reliance on large-scale transportation.

Interestingly, the rise of remote work and virtual living, amplified by the Metaverse, enhances the appeal of such physical hubs. With more individuals spending significant portions of their lives at home or in virtual spaces, local environments can become highly optimised for quality of life rather than daily commutes to distant workspaces. The Metaverse itself may extend the principles of the 15-Minute City into the virtual world, where individuals can access a digital economy and social spaces seamlessly from their digital homes, while still maintaining ties to their local, physical communities. In this dual framework, both the Metaverse and the 15-Minute City create environments where proximity—whether digital or physical—supports a more sustainable and human-centric way of living.

The combination of Metaverse development and concepts like the 15-Minute City illustrates the varied pathways that cities might take in the future—whether through hyper-localized, self-sufficient communities or sprawling digital hubs accessible from anywhere. As we rethink the very nature of physical and digital space, the traditional models of cities may become less relevant as the lines between home, work, and recreation blur further.

We are now standing on the cusp of a paradigm shift that extends beyond online shopping, video conferencing, or movie streaming. The Metaverse presents the possibility of recreating places and spaces online, approximating the experience of physical cities. In the Metaverse, where one's initial location becomes irrelevant, cities will assume a global character from their inception. This raises the question of whether the demise of cities as we know them is on the horizon. While it is possible that residential spaces may shrink, and urban areas may transform into service hubs rather than business centres, the broader implications of the Metaverse on urban landscapes remain to be seen.

The advent of the internet initially sparked the notion that location held diminished importance, a concept later proven incorrect. As we transition into the Metaverse era, the significance of physical location in the short term remains evident, with cities continuing to thrive and potentially expanding as centres of technology and innovation. However, as the level of realism in virtual environments intensifies, the allure of the physical world may gradually diminish.

A current example of this shift in the level of immersion and human co-presence is watching a movie in a Metaverse cinema populated by avatars. There are a number of applications that allow you to create your own cinema screens, invite friends, or even open the experience to the public, allowing for a shared viewing experience in a virtual environment (Figure 7.3).

FIGURE 7.3
A concept cinema in the Metaverse complete with avatars. Credit Authors.

Exiting the cinema and entering the Metaverse, the Cities of Tomorrow will be towering metascapes, digital in nature, composed of binary code rather than physical materials. These cities will be ever-changing and adaptable, serving as hubs for innovation, social interaction, education, retail, entertainment, and transportation. Teleport centres will act as directories of activities, providing shortcuts to popular destinations, they maybe come the new search engine, not on a 2D screen but in fully occupied three-dimensional space.

In physical cities, navigation requires either a paper map or a mobile device linked to a Global Positioning System (GPS) to track one's location and provide directions to the desired destination. However, the Metaverse is virtually boundless, necessitating a new type of navigation system. The intermediate destinations need not be known as teleportation between worlds is instantaneous. Although a few generations away, these digital cities are arguably the future of human habitation. Physical cities may experience a decline in the level of services provided, with a potential shift in focus away from public transportation and toward essential services such as food and local amenities. While this could be perceived as a dystopian future for physical cities, it may also represent the next step in human evolution, transitioning into the realm of digital existence and the concomitant development of digital cities—digital habitation.

Security

Security will be tight in the most popular Metaverse environments. As today, there will be terms and conditions to sign before entry, much like a theme park, while on the sidelines there will be areas with less security—frontier worlds within the future established Metaverse. This split does open up a number of key questions in society going forward. If our digital worlds are going to be all-consuming, what happens to those refused entry? Will the Metaverse be divided into a series of essentially private members clubs with a monthly membership fee? Will it be open and free for all, or will it be a service provided by a country's government and become a service linked to our current national passports?

Assuming that the Metaverse is subject to terms and conditions, the enforcement and policing of those terms become pertinent considerations. Will all actions and conversations be recorded and potentially used as evidence in the event of a breach? Additionally, the existence of security patrols and a Metaverse police force raises questions. How will the terms and conditions address illegal or harmful content, as well as content deemed inappropriate for families? It is important to note that many aspects of the Metaverse are still in flux, and there is the possibility of alternative worlds or realms designed for activities suitable for individuals over the age of 18. This in turn opens up discussions regarding whose terms, cultures, and laws would govern these worlds. Furthermore, the concept of a nation-state having its own Metaverse, one where citizens abide by national laws and morals and access to other Metaverse worlds is restricted, presents a possibility that reflects the current situation of the internet, where certain applications are only accessible in specific countries due to national regulations. As we write, Instagram is banned in China, and TikTok is going through the courts in America, heading towards a potential ban—apps are becoming fragmented due to national laws and culture. The Metaverse could go down the same route, losing the potential to bring people together in a global space.

To add a moment of darkness to the future—the potential for "Metaverse Wars" raises concerns. Drawing from the example of the terrorist attack on "30 Days in Active Worlds," it is conceivable that a rogue nation-state or terror group could target and disrupt a country's Metaverse infrastructure in the future. Consequently, the Metaverse may be accorded the same level of protection as a nation's undersea internet cables, electricity infrastructure, or transport networks.

Though uncharted, the broader scope of the Metaverse can be anticipated. Similar to all future developments, our digital identity and its safeguarding will assume greater importance. We have become accustomed to unlocking our devices with biometric features such as fingerprints and facial recognition. The next frontier is iris scanning, regarded as one of the most secure methods of verifying our identity. Each individual possesses unique and intricate iris patterns, making replication challenging. Iris scanners employ near-infrared light to capture high-resolution images of the iris. These images are then compared to stored records for authentication purposes. Iris scanners can distinguish between living and non-living tissue, rendering the use of fake irises ineffective for unlocking purposes. This concept of distinguishing between living and non-living tissue is particularly noteworthy as it holds implications for differentiating between humans and robots, thus blurring the boundaries between future technology and the science fiction depicted in films like "Blade Runner." While this may seem like a distant futuristic vision, it is already becoming a reality. At the time of writing, a company is actively travelling the world, engaging in iris scanning initiatives as part of a new currency system known as World Coin (WLD).

It is noteworthy that the company does not collect any personally identifiable information but rather employs this data with the objective of establishing a database and financial transaction system that serves the purpose of verifying whether an individual is indeed a human being, a concept they refer to as "proof of personhood." It does not verify a person's identity but instead specifies a unique humanness. To date, 12 million individuals have verified their humanness at an Orb (their scanning device) with each participant set to receive a certain number of World Coin tokens. It is important to recognise that within the context of the Metaverse, Orb scans would be ineffective, as avatars' eyes are digital in nature. However, this technology is fully functional within the confines of a headset or any digital device being utilised. Consequently, it is conceivable that in the future, accessing the Metaverse, accepting its terms and conditions, or confirming payment of a monthly subscription may necessitate an automated iris scan as a prerequisite. The future may be secure via biometrics, but it is also one where we are tracked and tagged across all our digital activities.

Conclusion

The initial industrial revolution harnessed the elements of water and steam to automate production. The subsequent revolution incorporated electric power, enhancing efficiency and broader manufacturing capabilities. The third revolution entailed the integration of information technology, utilising computers to accelerate and diversify the supply chain. We now stand on the threshold of a Fourth Industrial Revolution, as the World Economic Forum termed, characterised by the convergence of technologies blurring the boundaries between the physical, digital, and biological realms. This revolution encompasses AI and novel economic models where the distinction between humanity and technological augmentation matures, seamlessly integrating with the digital domain. It heralds a post-human revolution, enabling immersive experiences and digital habitation in three-dimensional digital worlds (Figure 7.4).

FIGURE 7.4
Digital habitation. Credit Authors.

This impending revolution brings with it a multitude of uncertainties, perhaps exceeding those of any preceding revolution. While it may disrupt workplaces and replace specific jobs with automation, it simultaneously presents opportunities for creating new employment activities and previously unimaginable experiences.

The companies of today will need to adapt to these transformative changes, in the same ways that companies needed to adapt to the previous industrial and technological revolutions. We have witnessed a limited manifestation of this adaptation with the widespread adoption of the internet. Internet-based technology has become so ubiquitous that it is almost difficult to conceive of a time when we lacked instant access to a vast repository of information. Yet it is only a few decades ago that access to almost any information required visits to local libraries to consult physical books.

Technology is moving fast.

The future is a mosaic of the physical and the digital. It is one of a multitude of Metaverses with our avatars inhabiting this digital landscape alongside our physical bodies—digital habitation. It is beyond "twins" with the real world linked to the digital; no longer a new frontier but a new reality of living in the cities of tomorrow—cities in the Metaverse.

Index

Note: Locators in *italics* represent figures.

For Product Safety Concerns and Information please contact our EU representative GPSR@taylorandfrancis.com Taylor & Francis Verlag GmbH, Kaufingerstraße 24, 80331 München, Germany